If You Knew
Then
What I Know
Now

··········

Ryan Van Meter

Sarabande  Books
LOUISVILLE, KENTUCKY

Managing Editor
Sarabande Books, Inc.
2234 Dundee Road, Suite 200
Louisville, KY 40205

Library of Congress Cataloging-in-Publication Data

Van Meter, Ryan, 1975-
  If you knew then what I know now / by Ryan Van Meter. -- 1st ed.
    p. cm.
  ISBN 978-1-932511-94-9 (pbk. : alk. paper)
  1. Van Meter, Ryan, 1975---Childhood and youth. 2. Authors,
American--21st century--Biography. 3. Gay men--United States--
Biography. I. Title.
  PS3622.A585495Z46 2011
  814'.6--dc22
  [B]
                                        2010025148

Cover and text design by Kirkby Gann Tittle.

Manufactured in Canada.
This book is printed on acid-free paper.

Sarabande Books is a nonprofit literary organization.

 The Kentucky Arts Council, the state arts agency,
supports Sarabande Books with state tax dollars and
federal funding from the National Endowment for the
Arts.

Dedication to come

First

. . . . .

Ben and I are sitting side by side in the very back of his mother's station wagon. We face glowing white headlights of cars following us, our sneakers pressed against the back hatch door. This is our joy—his and mine—to sit turned away from our moms and dads in this place that feels like a secret, as though they are not even in the car with us. They have just taken us out to dinner and now we are driving home. Years from this evening, I won't actually be sure that this boy sitting beside me is named Ben. But that doesn't matter tonight. What I know for certain right now is that I love him, and I need to tell him this fact before we return to our separate houses, next door to each other. We are both five.

Ben is the first brown-eyed boy I will fall for but will not be the last. His hair is also brown and always needs scraping off his forehead, which he does about every five minutes. All his jeans have dark squares stuck over the knees where he has worn through the denim. His shoelaces are perpetually undone, and he has a magic way of tying them with a quick, weird loop that I study and try myself, but can never match. His fingernails are

1

ragged because he rips them off with his teeth and spits out the pieces when our moms aren't watching. Somebody always has to fix his shirt collars.

Our parents face the other direction, talking about something, and it is raining. My eyes trace the lines of water as they draw down the glass. Coiled beside my legs are the thick black and red cords of a pair of jumper cables. Ben's T-ball bat is also back here, rolling around and clunking as the long car wends its way through town. Ben's dad is driving and my dad sits next to him, with our mothers in the back seat; I have recently observed that when mothers and fathers are in the car together, the dad always drives. My dad has also insisted on checking the score of the Cardinals game, so the radio is tuned to a staticky AM station and the announcer's rich voice buzzes out of the speakers up front.

The week before this particular night, I asked my mother, "Why do people get married?" I don't recall the impulse behind my curiosity, but I will forever remember every word of her answer—she stated it simply after only a moment or two of thinking—because it seemed that important: "Two people get married when they love each other."

I had that hunch. I am a kindergartener, but the summer just before this rainy night, I learned most of what I know about love from watching soap operas with my mother. She is a gym teacher, and during her months off, she catches up on the shows she has watched since college. Every summer weekday, I couldn't wait until they came on at two o'clock. My father didn't think I should be watching them—boys should be outside, playing—but he was rarely home early enough to know the difference, and according to my mother, I was too young to really understand what was going on anyway.

What I enjoyed most about soap opera was how exciting and beautiful life was. Every lady was pretty and had wonderful hair, and all the men had dark eyes and big teeth and faces as strong as bricks, and every week, there was a wedding or a manhunt or a birth. The people had grand fights where they threw vases at walls and slammed doors and chased each other in cars. There were villains locking up the wonderfully haired heroines and suspending them in gold cages above enormous acid vats. And, of course, it was love that inspired every one of these stories and made life on the screen as thrilling as it was. That was what my mother would say from the sofa when I turned from my spot on the carpet in front of her and faced her, asking, "Why is he spying on that lady?"

"Because he loves her."

In the car, Ben and I hold hands. There is something sticky on his fingers, probably the strawberry syrup from the ice cream sundaes we ate for dessert. We have never held hands before; I have simply reached for his in the dark and held him while he holds me. I want to see our hands on the rough floor, but they are only visible every block or so when the car passes beneath a streetlight, and then, for only a flash. Ben is my closest friend because he lives next door, we are the same age and we both have little brothers who are babies. I wish he were in the same kindergarten class as me but he goes to a different school—one where he has to wear a uniform all day and for which there is no school bus.

"I love you," I say. We are idling, waiting for a red light to be green; a shining car has stopped right behind us, so Ben's face is pale and brilliant.

"I love you too," he says.

The car becomes quiet as the voice of the baseball game shrinks smaller and smaller.

"Will you marry me?" I ask him. His hand is still in mine; on the soap opera, you are supposed to have a ring, but I don't have one.

He begins to nod, and suddenly my mother feels very close. I look over my shoulder, my eyes peeking over the back of the last row of seats that we are leaning against. She has turned around, facing me. Permed hair, laugh lines not laughing.

"What did you just say?" she asks.

"I asked Ben to marry me."

The car starts moving forward again, and none of the parents are talking loud enough for us to hear them back here. I brace myself against the raised carpeted hump of the wheel well as Ben's father turns left onto the street before the turn onto our street. Sitting beside my mom is Ben's mother who keeps staring forward, but I notice that one of her ears keeps swiveling back here, a little more each time. I am still facing my mother, who is still facing me, and for one last second, we look at each other without anything wrong between us.

"You shouldn't have said that," she says. "Boys don't marry other boys. Only boys and girls get married to each other."

She can't see our hands but Ben pulls his away. I close my fingers into a loose fist and rub my palm to feel, and keep feeling, how strange his skin has made mine.

"Okay?" she asks.

"Yes," I say, but by accident my throat whispers the words.

She asks again. "Okay? Did you hear me?"

"Yes!" this time nearly shouting, and I wish we were already home so I could jump out and run to my bedroom. To be back here in the dark, private tail of the car suddenly feels wrong so Ben and I each scoot off to our separate sides. "Yes," I say again, almost normally, turning away to face the rainy window. I feel her turn too as the radio baseball voice comes back up out of the quiet. The car starts to dip as we head down the hill of our street; our house is at the bottom. No one speaks for the rest of the ride. We all just sit and wait and watch our own views of the road—the parents see what is ahead of us while the only thing I can look at is what we have just left behind.

Lake Effect

. . . . .

I don't understand why he calls it a houseboat. It doesn't look like a *house,* and it doesn't look like a *boat.* What it looks like is a white box with windows cut out of the sides, railings clamped all around, and deck chairs tossed on the roof. The whole thing bobs in the lake, tethered to a dock post by a soggy green rope. Inside, everything is brown. The walls are covered in plastic panels printed with a wood-grain design, as if to remind us that wood floats and it's perfectly reasonable that we're loaded on this box for the next six days, instead of at home in an actual house. He, my Dad, is one of three Dads for whom this trip is now an annual thing, the third summer in a row that these college friends have brought along their elder sons for a week of fishing on a giant lake—this year, in Minnesota.

The kitchen in the houseboat is brown tile instead of brown carpet. I'm eleven years old and standing in front of the sink, washing every dish from the cupboards. The Dads and the other Sons are sitting on the slick white top of the boat, a deck on the roof above me. The sunset is beautiful, they keep telling me, but I keep doing the dishes, which is taking a lot longer than anyone would have guessed. We've already unpacked, already uncoiled the rope linking us to shore, already buzzed out across the water, turned off the engine, and started our slow drift around the lake in whatever direction the waves and wind push us.

Even though I've endured two previous trips, something about this houseboat idea unsettled me as soon as I heard about it. Maybe the intimacy of all of us aboard one small vessel, three Dads and three Sons in too close quarters? When my Dad announced our plan, I tried suggesting how disastrous my habit of sleepwalking might be on a houseboat, the way I could silently slip into the dark water before anyone noticed I wasn't tucked inside my sleeping bag anymore. This was unconvincing because, to his knowledge, I'd only sleepwalked once—when I was five and stood in the hallway snoring and peeing in a corner before shuffling back to bed—and because it hadn't happened since then, he wasn't worried.

I also hate fishing, but that's never worked, so I didn't bother bringing it up. I've always hated fishing because it's boring. For that first trip, I was simply excited by the fact that I was going somewhere on my own with Dad—no little brother or Mom. And I was so intrigued by the special pants required for trout fishing that I forgot about the fishing part. The waders looked like green, rubber overalls, and as soon as my Dad returned from the hunting store with a pair for me, I wiggled into them and started sliding my slick feet across the carpet, pretending I was figure skating. Besides wearing special pants, trout fishing also involved special rules, which he told me at home before the trip, and again on our first cold morning as we all walked with our poles and stepped down the river bank. I plunged into the frigid stream, the pants suddenly sucking at my body, and as the pressure of the water squeezed my legs and crotch, I fidgeted and tried to pretend I didn't already need the bathroom.

The rules were that we had to wait until a bell sounded before casting our lines. A game warden would watch us. The clear water streamed by as I shivered, and at the opposite bank, root-beer-colored trout darted in the current. Men in their own sucking pants stood in the water around me, their poles raised and patient. Somewhere in my waders, there was a sudden small coldness like I was leaking.

Sometimes I don't act the way boys are supposed to: in a high, panicked voice, I told my Dad about my waders. I felt the eyes of the other men turn to us. "Your pants are fine," he said, keeping his own voice low, his head still, his face calm. I had the feeling I'd done something wrong, and the anxiety snagged at me, forcing my leaking legs to shudder. My shaking fingers unlocked my fishing line. Before I knew it, I reflexively dipped my pole back and cast out to the opposite bank, the lure flying perfectly—in a way it never did from my arm—plunking down in the glittering cloud of fish under the water; they scattered and disappeared.

"What are you doing?" my Dad asked, dark lines creasing his forehead. I shook my head and tried to explain, but my voice wasn't working.

The rushing sound of the water grew loud like headphones turned up too high. I couldn't remember how to reel in my line, and I couldn't help but just stare at the thin, white wire that spanned the width of the stream connecting me to my mistake. Every man's eye in the water pointed at me, except my Dad's. The strange men groaned, whispered to each other, sighed. My stiff fingers finally snapped down the catch on my pole, and I quickly wound in the line, cranking the lever, hoping the fish would ignore my lure and that the warden wasn't watching. As soon as my hook lifted from the water, the bell went off. But the fish were already gone.

"You're not done with those yet?" Jim, one of the Dads asks, as he pushes open the sliding glass door of the houseboat kitchen and steps inside.

"I'll be done in a minute," I say. My fingertips are fat and numb, whitening and wrinkling, but I don't care. The evening sky is dark by now, and the square window above the sink is like a mirror; the yellow kitchen light puts my reflection up there, a small mouth drawing a tight line across a white face. Behind me, I see Jim bent over and rooting around in a cooler. He cradles a can of beer in the crook of his elbow, and digs around for two more. Three beers, three Dads.

Jim is the oldest of the three by just a year or two, though he doesn't look it. He actually doesn't act or dress much like a Dad either—or at least not like any of the Dads I know—the ones who wear T-shirts dotted with house paint and furniture stain, or ripped jeans smeared with car grease, like mine. Jim wears clothes like the popular boys at my middle school, the ones who live on the other side of the highway in the sprawling subdivisions with names. Polo shirts with flipped-up collars, plaid shorts, deck shoes. In clothes like those, with his carefully combed hair and his trimmed brown beard, he never looks ready to fish, but he still fishes anyway.

"Your dad says you're not playing baseball this year? Jimmy's missing a game this week, and it's killing him." In the window, I watch him yanking on a can of soda, trying to separate it from its clear plastic ring. Jim's son is also named Jim, but everybody calls him Jimmy. The third son on the boat with us is Eric. Jimmy and Eric live close enough to each other to be good friends. Because I only see them about twice a year, each trip it's like I'm meeting two brand-new boys.

I rub my sponge back and forth on the rim of a plate until it squeaks, and then it gets quiet enough to hear the dish-soap bubbles popping rapidly. I shrug to Jim.

"Well, Jimmy's pitching again. He loves it," he continues, and I turn around to finally face the real him, instead of the reflected one. He's holding three beers and a can of orange soda, and the hair on the backs of his hands is slicked down and shiny. Boys, like men, are supposed to want to do things like throw baseballs and catch fish. What do you call a boy who doesn't?

He slides the door open again with the toe of his shoe, and steps through it. "You don't even have to wash those in the first place, you know. You could just come on up."

"I know." With my sponge, I'm scrubbing hard between all the tines of all the forks. "I like it," I say. He doesn't know I keep refilling the sink with fresh hot water and new squirts of soap. What I like best about this chore is I'm the only one here that wants to do it, so it's mine, alone.

"Okay," he says, and he's gone. Last year, when we stayed in a cabin on another huge lake in Minnesota, I washed all the dishes on our first night too. I loved the cabin, especially being alone in it. When the Dads and Sons wanted to walk down to the slip and check out the boats, I stayed behind, pretending I was tired and needed a nap. Once they walked off far enough, I started my skipping. That summer, the year I was ten, I was convinced skipping got you across the house, the yard, the grocery store, or the baseball field better than either walking or running—though skipping publicly was strongly discouraged by my Dad. After a few skipped laps, I decided to pretend I was a Mom, a very busy woman, and this was my bustling house. I checked the beds, made sure the tub was scrubbed, jerked open each kitchen cupboard, removed every dish, washed and dried them, and stacked them back inside. During my charade, I talked aloud, scolding invisible children for standing under my feet while I cooked, warning my imaginary husband to stop asking if dinner was ready. Pretending to be characters like the busy Mom, or my other favorite, Beauty Pageant Winner, was something I did often, but only alone in my tree house or in my bedroom with the door closed.

I heard the Sons stomp up the porch stairs, and I had enough time to get into a mostly normal pose before they flung open the door. The Dads went off to buy some snacks at that little store, they said, the one I knew sold groceries *and* live worms. We decided to figure out the sleeping arrangements, and began wheeling around the extra rollaway beds, two of them, both folded in half and closed up.

During that second trip, the age difference between the Sons and me wasn't as obvious as the summer on the houseboat. The only noticeable difference in the cabin was simply that when my Dad wasn't around, I skipped and pretended I was a mother, while when the Sons weren't under the watch of their Dads, they moved furniture, and wondered if there was a way to sneak out at night to walk around the lake and look for girls.

Jimmy was all brown legs and arms, with long hands and feet like flippers. His skin and hair had the same goldenness of the lifeguards at the country club pool where I spent summer afternoons calling my parents from a pay phone, pleading to be picked up and taken home. Eric was a squattier, twitchier boy, with round cheeks and wide, light eyes. His rough hands would grab my shoulders and jerk and pull at me for a joke. He fiddled with any object that happened to be in front of him and often broke things without meaning to.

Eric perched himself on top of one of the beds to talk about wrestling, a popular topic for the Sons. The beds were crammed together at a right angle, forming a corner in the middle of the largest part of the cabin floor. Jimmy stood beside the other one, and I stood in front of them, pretending I knew what they were talking about.

"Did you see that awesome time he jumped off the ropes?" Eric asked, hands raised above his head. I'd missed the wrestler's name, but I pictured long hair, boots, a growling face, and a black unitard. Jimmy said, "Yeah, I think so. What happened again?"

"Man, it was so bad," Eric said. "He stood on the ropes and jumped down and clotheslined the bastard." To show us, Eric shot himself off the bed's edge and landed in the center of the room. The rollaway bed rocked on its small wheels, tipped forward, and the steel frame slammed on my left foot's big toe before I thought to move out of the way.

The pain shocked my bare foot, the toenail felt instantly loose and wet, and I knew that once the mattress was lifted, there would be a splatter of red across the floor, like ketchup packets squished underfoot across the school cafeteria tiles. I cradled my foot in my lap, squeezing it as hard as I could while tears fell out of my eyes. Jimmy and Eric stood silently with open-mouthed stares, wondering if they would be blamed. They couldn't believe I was sobbing, wailing like a girl and rocking with pain, all over a smashed toe.

The Dads returned with their snacks and found me laid across the floor, a dishcloth stuffed with ice cubes balanced on my red foot. There wasn't blood after all, though the nail was somehow very shiny, already dented and lavender. My Dad leaned over me while the other Dads examined the scene—by then the rollaway beds were standing against the cabin wall—and interrogated the witnesses. My Dad's fingers kept getting too close to the toe as he examined it. "Don't touch it," I warned, pulling it out of his hands. "You're fine," he said. An hour later, after the tears dried and my chin stopped vibrating, I limped dramatically to the bathroom, and limped the same way back to bed. The next morning, as we set off for a day of fishing for pike, the pointy fish in the lake that sparkled like chrome, the toe was purple and horrible. I hobbled to the motorboat, one sneaker on, the other dangling from my hand by the laces, because the idea of shoving the giant toe into a shoe made me swoon. "You're fine," he said again. "Just get in the boat."

Somehow, in just a year, the age difference between us now stretches out wide and obvious. Their bodies have changed, though I look the same: short, skinny, pale—a doll with a head too big for its body. Eric is even more solid, an efficient mass of energy and force with a line of dark fuzz curving along his upper lip. He barrels across the deck, he and his Dad grabbing each other, clamping necks into surprise headlocks, their knuckles grinding out noogies. Jimmy is grown up too, long and lean, not

gawky anymore but tall enough so his gold flipper feet fit the
ends of his legs. The Sons also both have leg hair.

If there is one thing I can enjoy about these trips, it's
watching and being this close to older boys—curiosities to a boy
who hardly looks or acts like one. This year I'm following Jimmy
around, watching intently as he does whatever he does. When
he fishes, I fish too, sometimes so focused on the mechanics
of his hands turning the crank on his pole, I forget to reel in
my own line. When he and Eric swim in the lake, leaping off
the roof, I station myself up there too with my stack of library
books. As much as I usually love reading about twin babysitting
sisters and haunted dollhouses, I can't keep my eyes off Jimmy's
flat body as he climbs the ladder and yanks up his soaking trunks
before bending and jumping again—the deep splash I can't see
but can imagine.

I've also got my Walkman with me, and a satchel full of
tapes. I know which ones to listen to in front of the Sons and
Dads, and which to reserve for my bunk bed. *Disney's Favorite
Songs*, Volumes One and Two, for example, are bunk tapes.
However, another one, the soundtrack to a rated-R movie that
I've never seen, is a public tape. It's music that other boys my
age would actually listen to. I like all the songs except the last
one—a loud insistent track with harsh, unintelligible lyrics. I
fast-forward through it so I can flip over the tape and start again
at the beginning with my favorite, The Pointer Sisters. On our
third morning, I sit at the kitchen table listening to my tape;

Jimmy picks up the empty case, unfolds the little booklet, and asks to listen to the last song.

I almost tell him he won't like it, it's the worst one, but before I can he says, "I like this band." I hand him my headphones. With the cord strung across the plastic wood tabletop, I press PLAY and watch his face as he listens; his head begins to nod as the rough beat begins to pound. I suddenly love the song without even hearing it because I love the way Jimmy listens to it. He asks to hear it again as soon as the final notes fade in his ears, and I manage the buttons, rewinding the tape and guessing the place where the song will start. "Go back," he says. "A little more." Then, "There. That's it," when we find the silent gap. He listens again and again.

For the rest of the trip, he'll listen to this song after I hold up the headphones to him and swing them side to side like a hypnotist's pocket watch. "Jim-mee? Don't you want to hear your song again?" I'll ask, high and cloying. When he agrees, I'll perform a look of exasperation, shake my head but also smile, and work the buttons to cue it up. Though he doesn't, if he were ever to turn me down, I know I'd feel a hard release of disappointment. Each time, the cord of the headphones connects us, the power streaming from my hands to his ears, and he is dazed by the rhythm while I scrutinize his face, music rippling across it.

The days pass on the houseboat, one the same as the next until one afternoon something across the lake catches my Dad's attention. He rushes in from the deck, crosses the kitchen where I'm seated at the table, and unzips his duffel bag. He runs across the kitchen again, this time clutching his spyglass, his small, handheld telescope. I love this telescope, though I'm not allowed to use it without his permission because it's expensive. In fact, its smooth bronze tubes and glass lenses weigh so heavily in my hands, it actually *feels* expensive.

But what he's looking at now, I have no idea. Usually we only look through the telescope at night, pointing it at the stars or the moon with its dark patches like birthmarks—one of us finds something bright and flashing in the sky and then passes it to the other one to share. He and the other Dads hunker now behind the railings and take turns, one eye looking through the telescope with the other one squeezed shut. They point, grip each other's shoulders and snicker, until one of them whispers something, and my Dad lets out a huge laugh, an explosion that seems to reach over the water.

He never laughs that way at home. There, he's the quiet one compared to my mom, my younger brother, and me, and he's always telling us he can't hear the news or his baseball game.

Leaving my books and Walkman in the kitchen, I tiptoe across the boat and hop into my bunk bed. There's a small window with a stiff, pleated curtain Velcro-ed over it. My fingers peel it back slowly, trying to keep the snagging sound quiet enough that it won't wake Jimmy from napping in the bunk above me, one of his feet hanging over the side, his breathing soft and constant like the rhythm of the lake waves. Far off in the frame of the window, a sailboat floats, small, white and shining. A woman stands at the prow, her long yellow hair hanging down.

From this far away, her skin is so orangey that I think she's wearing a bathing suit like my Mom's, one that covers her whole torso. But when I notice the dark blue wrapped around her lower part, I understand that she's wearing a bikini, just not all of it. Jimmy and Eric will want to see this—even though without a telescope, her nudity is completely featureless—so I stand up and look over the lip of the mattress. Jimmy's mouth is open and dark, his limbs are thrown over his sleeping bag. Before I wake him, I wonder what I will say about the naked woman and worry it will be wrong. Once, a kid I knew from school who lives in my neighborhood showed me a magazine of his Dad's filled with pictures of naked women. We squatted in the woods behind my house, and he turned the pages. One of the images was of a lady lying back on a floor, her knees bent, her legs parted. The neighbor pointed between them, glanced at me for my reaction. In a quiet, drawn-out voice I told him it looked disgusting. He grimaced and rolled up the magazine. The next day at school, the other boys in our class teased me for what I called the naked woman.

In my bunk, I smooth the curtain back in place so the woman disappears, though I still hear the Dads ogling her. What would Jimmy say about the naked woman if he were here instead of me? I prop myself up with pillows and watch his elegant foot as he dozes, knowing I could reach it if I lifted my hand. I want Jimmy to like me. I want to be like Jimmy, or I want to be Jimmy. Or I want to touch Jimmy.

Later that evening, we're all on the roof doing nothing. The naked woman's sailboat has drifted off to its own cove. A dark edge of trees reaches across the lake on one side of the boat, and on the other is a straight line of water drawn across the horizon. Above that blue line, the sky is pink and the red sun has been sitting in the same spot for hours. Eric and Jimmy are fishing, while the Dads sip early beers sitting in a row, Eric's Dad and my Dad in chairs, and Jim laid out on a chaise lounge wearing only his baseball cap and swimming trunks. I'm pretending to read the library book that's open in my lap.

The soft waves rock the boat in a lulling way that makes me sleepy. Eric's losing interest in fishing. Nothing's biting, not even a nibble. He turns and faces the dull sun, its color seeping down to touch the water. "Red sky in morning, sailors take warning. Red sky at night, sailor's delight." His Dad nods at him, which is probably who he heard that from—the saying I don't understand. This is another one of those things, like the naked magazine, that means something to them but not to me.

Jimmy feels the tug of a fish down below, starts shouting and pulling, his pole bending like the curve of a hook. He turns the crank. The fish must be fighting because Jimmy struggles against it, his big feet braced against the white railing, his whole body arching back. I'm mesmerized. There seems to be an impossible amount of line left to reel in, like Jimmy's pulling this fish in from miles away. Suddenly, a splashing sound, Jimmy cranks furiously, the fish is suspended at the end of the pole, twisting and thrashing. He hangs there, not that big but not small either, and Jimmy hands his pole to Eric so he can rip the hook out of its mouth.

"I don't want to clean any more fish today," Jim says. His eyes are closed. His hands cradle his own head as he dozes on the lounge. Jimmy says something to protest, then gives up easily, and continues fiddling with the fish. He and Eric talk about what kind it is, names I don't really register because, without being entirely conscious of it, I've been staring at Jim's bare chest. There's brown hair covering it, which starts in the divot at the root of his neck then spreads over the twin circles as wide as dinner plates between his armpits. His flat belly is covered in hair too. Pushed to the left and right of his chest, his nipples are smaller circles and dark red. In his arms, tough muscles like embedded baseballs roll up and down as he adjusts his body in his sleep. There's a second splash, which is probably Jimmy tossing his fish back to the lake, but I can't be sure because my eyes are stuck.

"Ryan," my Dad says. "Stop it."

Jim opens his eyes and sees mine pointing his direction. Eric's Dad and both Sons look over at me too. I freeze in my spot on the floor, looking back at my Dad until I can't stand his eyes. *Don't do that,* he mouths silently before I look away, and the fact that he can't say his words weights them.

My eyes fall to my crossed legs, staring at the book I've inadvertently closed, but I don't need to look up to know they are all searching me for whatever I've been told to quit. Nose picking, scab picking, hands in pants—I try imagining something objectionable but still not as awful as what I've actually done. My shame is solid, and I am immobile under the mass of it; my feet feel prickly like they've fallen asleep. All of us sit and wait for something, but it doesn't seem to arrive. Eric yawns and stretches. Jimmy throws his line out in the water again. Jim picks up his hat and scratches the crown of flat hair. Eric's Dad crumples an empty beer can. My Dad takes it from him. "Why don't you go get us three more?" he says to me, and suddenly my legs and feet operate again: I can move.

Below them, in the kitchen, I hear the scooting noises of deck chairs, their bare heels bumping across the ceiling from one side to the other. I wait for voices, for my Dad's explanation, but it doesn't come. Just more laughing, Dads and Sons, and then more cheering coming from Jimmy. From the window, I watch a golden fish rise out of the water like a miracle, dripping and spinning as the line hooked in his mouth lifts him into the air. Jimmy's got another one. The fish levitates a few seconds and then ascends out of view.

I've embarrassed my Dad on our trips before, so why does this feel different, more severe than casting out too early in a trout stream or being dramatic about a toe? I flip the lid off the cooler, dig my fingers into the ice, scoop up two handfuls of cubes, lift them dripping out the water, and release them sloshing back down. I was just looking at him. Why, if that was so embarrassing, didn't my Dad just stay quiet? And why did he have to say something in front of Jimmy?

I slump down on the brown tile and wrap my cold hands around the back of my neck. From this angle, all I can see in the window is the glowing blankness of pre-evening sky. There's so much water shimmering and vast in every direction. I want to drop silently and lose myself in it without fighting the way fish do when they're pulled into the air. I'd like to just step off the boat—it would be something my body wants to do, an accident, and nobody knows why.

Houseboat. There are some names for things that don't fit if I think about them too much. *Toenail. Cupboard. Hot dog.* How much does a thing have to resemble its word? *Butterfly. Boy.* They all looked at me when he said my name, they all wanted to see what I'd done this time. The same way those men looked at me with my line stretched across the water on that trout-fishing morning. Every eye was on me, except my Dad's. But I understand now that the men weren't just looking at me; they knew what kind of boy acted the way I did. What they wanted to find out was what kind of a man my father was. He spoke my name up there to keep from facing that look again.

I dig three beers out of the cooler. They sting my bare arm

as I rest them in an elbow crook, cradling them like Jim did. I somehow balance them, and if I slide my feet and go slow, I can make it up the ladder. There's suddenly no noise above me. They have quieted because they're listening, straining for the sound of my feet crossing the boat under them, the punch of my heels up the metal rungs of the ladder. I stop in my place and listen back, staring out the window. I remember Jimmy's fish, and I listen for that too, deciding I'll move again only when it slides from his fingers towards the water and splashes back into its own darkness.

Practice

· · · · ·

This is his deal: if I play baseball one more season, my Dad will buy me a color TV for my bedroom. I'm nine years old and standing in front of him, pulling at my room's red shag carpet with my toes while I listen to the terms of our agreement; it's the beginning of the summer right after third grade. As he talks, I nod my head slowly like it's heavy and look at my dresser where my record player sits and then at the shelf crammed with books and stuffed animals, trying to figure out where the TV should go. He clears his throat, and his voice gets grave and serious as he starts telling me my end of the bargain. I have to practice a lot, every day if possible, and I have to be good about it, which means no complaining or saying "it's too hot" or "later" or "wait" and most importantly, I must promise to really try.

"Do you know what I mean by trying?" he asks. He's sitting on my bed so his face isn't as high as it usually is.

"Uh huh," I say. My history with sports isn't long, but I've already got a reputation. I've attempted gymnastics, swimming lessons, soccer and two previous seasons of baseball. Every time, I'm the small kid who slouches at the quiet corners of the action, stands still and tries not to be noticed by the instructor, coaches, team members or spectators. I'm the player who's always reminded to concentrate, kick harder, run faster and keep my eye on the ball.

"Do we have a deal?" he asks.

Standing there, I lean my head to one side and try to decide if I like TV more than I hate baseball. "Yes," I say, finally.

He thinks we should shake on it, and we do. His rough hand is very big and in his grip, mine disappears.

I'm the only one in our house who doesn't like sports. My Mom is a PE teacher, and she played softball in college and also as a little girl, when she and her friends played any day it wasn't raining in an empty lot with old roof shingles for bases. My Dad used to be the football coach of the high school he works at, until he became the principal, and he also played softball in college, as first baseman. He has several stories about those games, including a particularly gruesome one that involves a line drive hit and a dislocated thumb that he discovered only when he felt something warm on his wrist. Even my five-year-old brother shows some talent for Tee-ball. But because the ball just sits there waiting for you to hit it no matter how many times you swing, I don't find him very impressive.

They keep thinking I must be good at something, we just haven't found the right game. It seems unbelievable that a boy wouldn't like sports. My problem with sports is you generally have to be outside to play them—especially baseball—and being outside is often too hot and also makes me sneeze. If I have to be outside, there are plenty of things I'd rather do that don't involve chasing after balls. Like lying on blankets spread in the shade with a picnic packed for one, pretending to read *Little Women*. He interrupts me when I'm in the yard like this, tossing me my glove, asking if I want to throw the ball around. Sometimes I wonder why he tries so hard or why, at those moments, he always thinks we need to practice.

We're in the back yard, practicing. The sun is hanging in exactly the wrong place so it shines in my eyes. This is our regimen: throwing the ball back and forth, fielding the ball and hitting pitches—but first, we warm up. As agreed by yesterday's handshake, I'm supposed to make certain I throw the ball hard and fast and also precisely, because even in the back yard, I should imagine I'm playing in a real game, and I'm throwing to get a hitter out. This is *trying*. I'm pretty good at it when I want to be. After what feels like ten thousand rounds, he says, "All right," and starts throwing the ball straight up as if it's a pop fly. I have to run around, search the sky and try to catch it. With the orange sun stuck in its spot though, I see the ball go up and then it's burned out in the light, falling to the grass. I start to complain but he gives me a look—flat lips and frozen eyes—to remind me of the no-complaining clause. I miss another one and stand there for a few seconds, trying hard not to look like a kid who wants to run away from home.

"Let's try something else for a while!" I make my voice sound excited.

He says okay and it's time for grounders, which are worse than pop flies. For these, he throws the ball sharp and quick so it bounces toward me. I hate these because you never know when the ball is going to bump off the ground to punch you in the face. Every time it comes at me, I think about my Dad's dead thumb and can't help but squeeze my eyes shut and blindly stretch out my glove, hoping the ball decides to bounce in.

"Don't be a pansy," he says. "You look like you're afraid of the ball."

I *am* afraid of the ball.

In our routine, practice ends with hitting. If my Mom's not busy, she squats behind our home plate to be catcher. This was her position when she was younger, so she actually has the metal mask and the special fat glove. Her old last name is still written across her glove in tall black letters, even though now she has the same name as everybody else in the house. If she's busy, he just throws the ball over the plate, and if I miss, I have to get it myself and throw it back.

This first practice after the agreement, she's busy. I miss four in a row and then he throws another, I swing, miss again, and drop my bat. I stomp around in the grass by the fence. The ball keeps rolling underneath it. I get down on my belly, squeeze my arm under the fence but the ball's not close enough. So I get back up, crouch on my knees, and sigh. "Hustle," he says. I'm up, running to the gate next to the house, running back down on the other side of the fence, then grabbing the ball, throwing it to him, running back through the gate, making sure it's latched, and hurrying to the plate and my bat and getting ready to swing. The sun rolls down the sky to stare from right behind my Dad's head; he glows as he winds up and throws. The ball blurs past.

In our house, besides my parents and the little brother who's always barging into my room, there's a dog we call Victor, a name that makes me think of an old man. He is brown and white and his face actually looks like an old man's with distant eyes, whiskers and snaggleteeth. Before my Dad got married to my Mom and before we—my brother and me—came around, he lived alone with Victor. Now Victor has to stay in the basement most of the time because he doesn't enjoy the way Garrett and I play with him—dressing him up in my mother's old nightgowns, whipping his tail for him side to side. He growls and shows us his teeth until we back away.

The only one of us the dog likes is my Dad. They play fetch in the yard sometimes. He needs a little coaxing to return the ball, but will keep chasing after it for hours. When my Dad and the dog are playing in the yard like that, or if my Dad is working out there, pushing his wheelbarrow around or cutting into the ground with his spade, and Vic is out there too, nosing the grass, I think about what our house was like before Garrett and I were born. I've seen the pictures of my parents' wedding, with their smooth, white faces and weird hairdos. Like the terrible thumb story and others they could tell, I want to know about their young lives. How did they know they wanted to be a Mom and Dad and how did we all come to live in this house—them, my brother, the dog, me?

One thing I do know about my Dad is he's a pretty serious guy. Also, he loves silence. When the Cardinals are playing, he listens intently to the games, reminding us to be quiet if we walk by singing songs. Besides baseball, and taking me to the library any time I ask—even on consecutive days when I read too fast—my Dad and I don't do much together because, other than books, we don't like the same things. He doesn't listen to records and dance in the basement or make potholders or watch *Mama's Family*. I don't like to mow or push around the wheelbarrow. And I know he's trying desperately to find something for us to share, which is why he tries to get me to play sports. My Dad believes in practice, the idea that if you work at something you're not necessarily very good at, if you keep throwing balls and catching them, you will get better. I will enjoy the game as much as he does, I just have to try.

We're in the backyard, practicing. It's a hot afternoon, he's just returned home from school. I have spent the whole day inside, watching soap operas with my Mom and rearranging the stuffed animals on my bookshelves. The heat is miserable, made worse because he's making me wear my bright white uniform pants, even though they are really only for games. Victor is out here with us, snout in the grass, but he must be somewhere on the other side of our yard, because I can't see him.

"Are we almost done?" I ask. Sweatdrops creep down my neck and under my shirt collar like red ants.

This is what he's talking about when he says I'm supposed to be "good" about practicing. We're working on grounders. One ball after another has skimmed my hesitant glove and hammered past me. I miss yet another one and sigh, letting my head hang back, my mouth flung open because I've had it. My arms are lifted, stay there one second, then fall down, hands hitting my sides.

"Come on," he says.

Before I can help it: "I'm sick of this."

"Ryan," he warns. We had a deal.

"I don't even want a TV anymore," I say, toeing the ball in the grass.

"You say that now. Just try."

"I do. I hate baseball."

The ball is still on the ground, in front of my feet. Facing me, he plants his hands on his hips, and we stare at each other like cowboys in a duel. He's wearing his old coaching shorts, the ones that used to be white, but now are grey. All over them are tiny specks and smears of color from all the things he's painted. The maroon dots are from the stairwell to the basement. Brown is the color of our house. Green is for the bridge we made together to stretch over the creek out back; we sunk the boards from one mud bank to the other, not knowing about the big storm that would wash it out that night. Not a single green-painted board was left the next morning. He's also wearing his old sneakers. They are so big I can stand in them and walk if I clench my toes and scoot the shoes along the ground without lifting my feet up; one day, he says, my feet will fill them, but at the moment that idea seems as impossible as multiplication tables.

"Come on," he says. "Pick up the ball."

"Why do we have to practice here if I have to still *go* to practice too?" The team has been practicing a few weeks now. Our first game is tomorrow. The ball just sits there, grass sticking up all around it. It could be a plastic Easter egg full of candy just waiting for me to find it.

"Ryan," he says, "I don't want to hear it. Pick up the ball." If I know what's good for me, I'll stop testing him.

I've been working on this trick. My coach's son—our team's pitcher—does this at practice. I lean down just a little and scoop with my straight arm and try to grab the ball with the glove quickly without bending all the way over. If my glove stays open in a cupped shape, I can get underneath it and just fling it to him in one swift motion. It's a new trick though and instead of the ball flying straight to him, it just rolls across the grass, about ten steps away from his sneakers and all the way over to the right. I stand still to see what will happen next.

He stomps forward, picks up the ball and turns. It shoots

out across our yard, high up like he hit a home run even though he only threw it. It flies up and then drops into the wooded part of our yard, the part with the creek where the bridge is supposed to be and the sewer drainpipe with its weird smell. "Go get it," he says, pointing, and then he walks to the house.

Suddenly everything is easier. Practice is over. I might be in trouble, but somehow I don't care. Once I find the ball, I can go back in, out of this heat. I trudge down the slope of the yard where the grass ends and the ground becomes covered in packed-down leaves and mud. Tall, skinny trees rise up and cover the whole area so it's quiet, except for the sound of my shoes. Victor digs at something in the dirt, and he looks up at me coming down into what he considers his territory. "Hi," I say, and wave so he knows I'm not a stranger he needs to devour. I'm just one of the kids who ruined everything, who came along and made him have to live in the basement and now I've even disrupted his silent investigation of a leaf pile. My ball is shoved in the crook of two tree roots. I dig it out and leave Victor to his sniffing.

I hike back to the house, heading for the garage. Crowds cheer from our driveway, so there must be a Cardinals game tonight. My Dad likes sitting outside on nights when a game is on. He's in his lawn chair, the same one he brings to my games so he can sit by himself in right field, near me, because I'm the right fielder. The radio blares on the concrete, an orange extension cord snaked out of our open garage. He's facing the street, waving a hand to neighbors who walk by. The radio announcer tells us what the pitcher is doing, how many strikes he throws, and how many balls. The voice is so loud my Dad can't hear me walk behind him to put the ball with the rest of my baseball stuff. He's drinking iced tea, there's a dark wet ring on the cement next to his chair where he's fitting the bottom of his glass in the same spot every time. Silently, I lay the ball down into the bowl of my glove, folding the leather over it, closing it up inside like a secret. He still can't hear me as I stand behind him watching him listen. The Cardinals are losing and one of them is batting with two strikes, but then he hits it and the announcer is excited, telling us that the ball flies over the head of the shortstop to a hole in the outfield. The batter makes it to second, it's a double, there's a chance now to even the score. My Dad sits up in his chair, his hands tensed, bunched into fists.

I know I should walk up to him. I know I should sit beside him on the cement and listen to his game. I should try harder when he practices with me and I should not give up so easily. I almost want to tap his shoulder and tell him I'm sorry but he doesn't like to be bothered when a game is on, so I tiptoe off, out of the garage, as the crowd chants their hero's name.

As much as I hate playing baseball, especially with the other kids all bigger and better than me, the season passes quickly. I daydream through most of the games anyway. When the other team is at bat, I stand in right field, far off from most of the drama. My Dad sits out there too in his lawn chair, the only spectator not sitting with the clapping parents behind home plate. He sits close by so he can remind me that the ball is coming. While the other kids lean in and taunt the batter, I find animals and funny faces in the clouds and examine the clover under my feet looking for one with four magic leaves. When our team is up, we sit on the bench in batting order. My spot is all the way down, third from last.

Between games, my Dad and I still practice at home even though the team practices at the park a couple of times a week. The skill I've developed most during these sessions with Dad is the ability to daydream during practice as well. I haven't gotten any better at playing baseball, but the routine is so reliable that I can think and think and think about more interesting things and still catch and throw balls.

One afternoon near the end of the season, with only four games left on our schedule, Dad and I are throwing the ball around in the front yard near the curb and I miss one; it rolls into the street and falls in the sewer. He's a little mad because we don't have that many balls, and that was a new one. I'm a little excited because now we can't practice. He stands over the mouth of the sewer, hands on his hips again, gazing into the opening like he'll actually see the ball in there even though it's too dark. I've got my glove off and I'm skipping to the house, nearly dancing I'm so happy. "Grab the flashlight," he says, and marches across the grass to the back yard.

Anything that goes down the sewer in the front of our house comes out of the big drainpipe over the creek behind our house. When it's raining, water gushes out like a spigot twisted all the way open. When I get down there with the flashlight, he's standing at the bottom of the hill, balancing his big body on some flat rocks. He's tall enough to peer into the opening of the pipe. I hand him the flashlight and start to run up the hill, but he calls my name.

"Eight feet at the most," he says. Pointing the beam of the flashlight into the pipe, he sees the ball about six feet in. I slide down and stand beside him, not tall enough to see inside the pipe or see the ball, or see through the shimmering webs full of annoyed spiders squinting out at him. He wants me to crawl in there.

Because he suggests it like it's no big deal, I have to act that way too, and just do it, without being a pansy or making yuck sounds. This is also trying—trying to help out, to be a good sport, to be a man about this. I climb up on him and he hoists me, his hands around my middle, lifting and pushing me headfirst into the pipe. It's dark and cool inside, and there's a small puddle of water trapped between each of the corrugated metal humps, and even though it's a little wider than my shoulders, I still have to scrunch myself up to move through. The smell inside is something like mud and something like spoiled milk so I'm breathing only through my mouth and pushing myself forward with the rubber toe edge of my sneakers, my knees bumping along the metal. His face is behind me, looking in and shining the flashlight. "See it?" he asks. His voice sounds tiny and far away. The ball is right in front of me with dark stuff smeared on it. My reaching arm moves through a net of spider webs and feels like I'm pulling on an invisible sleeve. I stretch out and my fingers slide off the slick side of the ball. Then I push myself in one more inch so I've got it, my palm pressing down on the ball's smooth skin and neat stitches like I'll never let it go. It's so black I can't see anything except the ball squeezed in my hand. But as much as it stinks and it's cold on my belly where my T-shirt is soaked and I want to slap the spiders dropping down their strings above my white legs, as much as I want to be a pansy, inside this drainpipe it's also somehow safe. I've found the place where I have control of the ball, where it can't humiliate me, where I am finally better at something than he is. No catching and throwing and no grounders. He knows I hate crawling around like this, but I know if I lie quietly enough and pretend I'm doing something brave, maybe we won't have to play this game anymore.

"You got it yet? You see it?" My Dad's yellow light wiggles over me. My arm is curled back; I cover the ball with my body.

"Almost," I tell him.

The last game of the season. I've somehow persevered and made it to the end. And even if our team wins today's game, we still can't make the play-offs. "So then why do we have to play?" I asked my Dad, and he told me to put my bat and glove in the car. In the last inning, I'm the second batter—the last time I'll ever bat in a game. I know if this were a library book or a movie, if someone was telling this as a story, this would be the swing when I hit a home run, tie the score and take us into extra innings, my teammates leaping from the bench and my Dad feeling huge and proud.

It's not a library book though. It's me, so I'm standing at home plate and the count is one ball and two strikes. The pitcher is this tall kid with such a suntanned face, he looks dirty. The catcher behind me has sweaty arms, little balls of water spread all over his skin. Dust rolls in waves across the field like my Mom snapping clean sheets across my bed. The foam cushions inside the batting helmet are soaked, the cold sponges pressing on my ears.

The pitcher stands still, then explodes into movement, leg bending up and arm going over like he's just come apart. His hand opens and the ball comes out and my eyes try to follow it, but it's spinning so fast the red stitches are blurred. It flies and comes at me as I'm thinking about practice with my Dad, how I have to hit this or go fetch it on the other side of our back yard fence. The ball drops in the air, falling and still flying, dropping and shooting above the ground by my front foot. It can't be a strike, it's too low, but it's fast and I don't know how close it is and I can't move quickly enough to get out of its way. The ball smacks me right against the round knob of my ankle joint, pushing my feet out from under me. I fall, my hands in the dust, the ball rolling, my aluminum bat clunking down—the handle knocking home plate with a metal pinging that vibrates in the stiff air.

The place on my bone where the ball hit vibrates too. Or maybe it's echoing so the pain hits me again and again, out to my toes and up my leg to my knee. My Dad is here suddenly, all the way from his lawn chair. He picks me up and helps me stand. Because he's always reading books, I want to ask him if a bone can echo—I'm betting he would know. My coach is also here, crouching in front of me. He knows my Dad is smart too because he's asking him the questions instead of me. Can he run the bases? Can he still play? My foot feels broken but it's not. I can wiggle everything. My Dad cradles my foot in his big hands, one wrapped around the ankle, the other around the top of my foot and down to the heel. He covers the part that hurts, the bone in there that's bumping with pain.

The coach's hand is on my shoulder. He's pulled his hat off and his hair underneath is wet and pressed down. I get a base because the pitcher hit me and my coach thinks I should take it. "Walk it off, you'll be fine," he says. One of my Dad's hands rubs my cheek, there's dirt clinging to a wet spot on my face. He's asking me the same questions that the coach asked him. Can I walk on it? Do I think I can take the base? I'm not saying any words, just shaking my head side to side like it's heavy.

My Dad's so smart he knows I can run the bases just fine

but he's not going to make me. In a few minutes, he will carry me to the grass behind the bench and hold a cold can of grape soda to my throbbing bone. Tomorrow, I'll limp dramatically behind him into Tipton's Appliances and pick out my new TV—one with beautiful silver knobs and plastic sides that look exactly like dark-stained wood. A deal is a deal. This summer, we've been trying to be certain kinds of men we probably weren't ever meant to be. And sitting together on the field, we both know I'm the only quitter here because he's trying much harder to be my Dad than I've tried to be his son.

Shivering in the dust, I don't look at his face or my coach or the boys on my team, all standing behind the dugout fence, or the catcher and the pitcher trading smirks, or the umpire peering over my coach's shoulder. At the moment, I can't even look at the clouds. This kind of focus is what he means when he tells me to keep my eye on the ball. Right now, the only thing I can watch are my Dad's hands wrapped around my ankle because I can't believe so much sting is already fading under just the heat of his squeeze.

Discovery

. . . . .

I'm not allowed to go back to that chicken coop for at least an hour. "Those hens can't lay with someone in there all the time," my grandmother says. "Someone" I know, means me, the eight-year-old boy known around here for barging into henhouses, at least during these summer weeks my brother Garrett and I spend with her and my grandfather. If she would let me carry a chair and table out there, as I've repeatedly suggested, and set up a comfortable area in the corner of the coop to watch from, then I wouldn't disturb the chickens with my constant excited arrivals—swinging open the plank door and stomping across the speckled floor, anticipating newly-made eggs.

Reaching under a dozing chicken in the small nesting boxes and finding an egg there is a miracle, one that happens several times a day—not nearly enough. It's like finding a five-dollar bill or a jewel on the sidewalk. The egg in my hand is warm, heavy, a singular whole thing, impossibly smooth and brown, the same color as the makeup sealed in tiny glass jars in my mother's medicine cabinet at home. To think that *this* comes out of a chicken is mysterious and somewhat sickening, but I crave the discovery, and sometimes when I push my hand under those nervous, feathered bodies and mistakenly imagine my fingertip slipping over polished eggshell, I actually gasp. When the hen flutters off, her egg-making concentration broken, and she leaves me with her bare nest, I generally call her a name I couldn't repeat in front of my grandmother.

But this afternoon, here in the kitchen, a warning has been made about the henhouse. I am to stay in here until right before dinner, until Garrett and Grandpa come in from the field, no matter what. Only then, when the tractor is back in the machine shed, and my grandfather is washing up, may I check on the eggs.

Other than stalking chickens, there's not much to do at the farm. After the four-and-a-half hour car ride, and our eager greetings once we arrive, I slowly remember the previous long summer visits, the quiet days stretching out in my head, hot and dull. This is a working farm, and that's what they do—my grandparents—ticking off the same list of chores one by one every day, whether little boys are here or not. Their mornings start in the dark hours before dawn when they sit at the kitchen table and he reads the Bible aloud before she cooks their breakfast. My grandfather then spends the rest of his day driving huge machines around, doing things to the soybean and hay fields that I don't understand. Garrett likes anything with an engine so he goes along. My grandmother tends to her garden and the chickens, sews, washes clothes, makes lunch, cleans it up and then makes dinner. This is a farm in the middle of nowhere—nowhere near toy stores or libraries —so far from everything that even their mailbox is on the wrong side of the road, as if no one here has ever seen the way it is supposed to be.

In the kitchen, dinner is underway. My grandmother is measuring rice, peeling carrots, sugaring a pie. She works so quickly and mechanically, without any words—the way she does almost anything—that she doesn't notice me sliding my feet across the blue linoleum and down the hall. I know enough not to try opening the big door to go outside, so I wander down to the bedrooms, looking for a distraction. In the room where Garrett and I sleep, my Dad's room when he was a boy in this house, I sit on the bed, bounce a little and stare longingly out the window through walnut branches at the chicken coop.

There's a large closet and rummaging through things might give a few minutes of pleasure. On the shelves, I expect to find old toys of my Dad's, thinking of the shelves of my own closet—hand-puppets, Candyland, my potholder loom—stuck there in the silent dark without me. And here is a Davy Crocket lunchbox, a glass jar packed with plastic soldiers, a metal car with doors that open, and strange orange numbered tags with barbed points that I'll find out later are pushed through the velvet of a cow's ear to mark them. On the bottom shelf, shoved beneath a lace tablecloth and a crocheted blanket is a large white box; inside it, wrapped in tissue paper, a blue dress.

Shaking it out, smoothing away wrinkles and laying it

across the carpet, I know immediately this is a dress for a girl, not a woman. The length is for a body about my height. Stiff navy satin with short puffy sleeves, wiggly gold designs threaded into the tight middle part—the pleated embellished bodice—cloth heavy and lush as I lift the skirt to trace the perfect stitches of the hem and peek underneath. My Dad has a sister, a tall regal woman named Aunt Karen, so maybe this is hers from a long time ago.

I throw my T-shirt into a sweaty lump in the corner, and standing in front of the mirror on the back of the bedroom door, I pull the dress over my head and my shorts, and see that *yes*, it does seem made for someone my size. The bottom hem just skims the carpet as I shift my weight left and then right, my eyes in the mirror watching the full skirt tilting like a bell. I gather the folds of the dress in my hands, the way the women do on *Little House on the Prairie*, and bustle around for a minute or two before the door opens.

My grandmother. She just stands there and keeps her hand on the knob. She doesn't say anything, only stares at me with her serious face—the same face she always wears.

"I found this," I say. My hands clasp each other behind my back. I look at the T-shirt wadded up on the floor near her feet, but she doesn't seem to notice it. The fact that I took off my T-shirt before I put on the dress makes me feel more embarrassed, as if I'm somehow exposed in front of her, though the dress covers me, neck to toes. Suddenly my arms feel cold and the trim encircling the collar scratches my neck. She stays there, utterly still, and doesn't speak.

I say, "It fits me," and sort of twist side to side.

"It does. It does," she says. Her lips press together, bunching up like my two handfuls of blue satin, and then she lets them go. "I was coming in here to see if you would set the table for Grandma."

She knows I love setting the table because she taught me how.

The fork goes on the left and that's easy to remember because *left* has an *f* in it, and *f* is for *fork*. The knife and spoon go on the right. The plate should always be an inch from the table's edge, which is two thumb widths. Water glass on the right of the plate, and just a little right of the knife's point. Tea for Grandma and Grandpa, milk for Garrett, water for me. Napkin folded in half in the center of each plate. We always pass to the right.

In the dining room, I walk behind each pushed-in chair, and check the settings I've laid out. Over and over, I circle the table, each time nudging a fork, straightening a napkin, tapping a glass or pushing the ceramic boy salt shaker just a little closer to his twin, the pepper girl. Butter dish, pickle bowl, a stack of sandwich bread on a plate, milk pitcher, everything is here. Hanging next to one of the long sides of the table, a wide mirror stretches across the wall. I can't get enough of watching myself, gazing at how I move and perform these tiny actions, which are somehow glamorous now instead of just chores. Because I'm wearing the blue dress.

And I love the feeling of the skirt on my legs, the cool slickness sliding over my skin, how the hem rustles over the carpet when I stop suddenly to fix a spoon. Or how dark the small sleeves look against my white arm. I love smoothing my hand down the crinkles of the bodice. And standing at a corner of the table, spinning on my heel, watching the dress open up wide and twist around my feet. The gold thread, the pleats, the tightness at my waist. I love touching my face when I'm wearing the dress because beautiful women touch their faces a lot when they want to be noticed. I even pick up one of the spoons and hold its end to my ear lobe, imagining it as a long silver earring.

Because wearing it has me spellbound, I don't hear the tractor rumbling down the big hill and through the gate toward the grey machine shed. They are coming in for dinner. In the doorway, my grandmother dries her hands on the white apron tied around her waist. She's wearing a housedress, a worn shapeless thing printed with small yellow flowers. It's neither as lovely nor as womanly as mine, but I still wish I could wear that one too.

"Thank you for helping," she says, standing in the watery light reflected off the mirror from the dinnertime sun.

"You're welcome," I say, curtsying like the women on TV.

Though we can't hear it from the house, my grandfather heaves and pulls on the giant machine shed door to close it. He and Garrett start marching up the gravel driveway toward the house.

My grandmother fidgets with her apron, her thumb rubs a stain near an embroidered leaf. "I expect you should change for dinner before your Grandpa gets here," she says. Something on the stove is boiling over, steam pushing up on the pot lid, froth escaping and sizzling against an orange burner coil. She ignores it. We look at each other, a woman in her dress, a boy in his, one of us on each end of a perfectly set table for four. Here is a secret we both helped make, and in this moment we feel it dropping fully formed down into each of our bodies, whole and heavy, where it will sit forever. I'm too young to know exactly why we're keeping the secret, but I know we're not going to tell anybody what she's just let me do. "You better scoot," she says.

The sun falls a bit lower behind the old barn. Silverware sparkles. My earring spoon isn't close enough to its knife but I can fix that later. "Okay," I say, hurrying to the bedroom as the hem of my dress whispers against the carpet.

Specimen

. . . . .

That first night I couldn't help imagining myself the way I thought they saw me—their view from the sky with X-ray vision cutting through the roof. There I was in my queen-sized bed, thirteen years old, staring at the ceiling with my blankets bunched under my chin in pale fists. I had nowhere to look but up. On one side of my bed was the window, and even with the blinds twisted shut, I could still see about an inch of black, threatening sky. On the other side was my door, with the margin of light at the bottom where I felt sure, at any moment, I'd see the shadows of their footsteps creeping in to yank me out of my world. Despite being desperately tired, I couldn't close my eyes either. If I fell asleep, I was a goner.

It didn't seem possible to be so scared by something on TV, especially a show I watched every week with my mother. And while the mystery show did freak me out a little sometimes— like the one with the haunted bunk-bed that left burn marks on your skin and even whispered *You're dead*—I still couldn't wait for a new episode every Wednesday night. My favorite part was when the host would appeal to us, the audience at home.

If you have any information regarding this case, please call the toll-free number on your screen. Paper faces of suspects with penciled eyes and shaded mouths flashed up. I memorized them and, in my mind, held them up to all the faces I encountered in a day, wishing the school janitor, my mustached geometry teacher or the grocery store bagger was a killer or thief I could identify and turn in.

But the show that night had been different. It was a special hour-long program about alien abductions, and at the beginning, I thought it was pretty ridiculous. How could the police arrest aliens? But as the stories unfolded, I started to become more and more afraid. Sitting Indian-style in front of the TV, I felt my teeth lock together and my eyes squeeze closed when the descriptions of the abductions got particularly horrible. Which was why I couldn't sleep. The aliens abducted some of the people on the show while they slept. And the part that had me most terrified was that the sleepers would actually wake up during their kidnappings. The aliens—silent, glowing and green—would surround their beds and the people would try to move or scream, but they had been paralyzed. Aliens had some eerie power over the body.

In the past, whenever I was frightened by scary movies or TV shows—or once, by a news alert that a serial child killer strangely named Michael Jackson was loose in our town—the only way I could sleep was to be with my parents in their bedroom. That arrangement began when I was very young, four or five, and awful nightmares would send me to sleep in their bed. But to be thirteen years old, and about to ask my mother—the only one in the house still awake at this late hour—to sleep with me felt embarrassing. Even so, I flung off my blankets, and from my bedroom, followed the light to the living room where I knew I'd find her, TV still on, in the yellow glow of the lamp beside her, bent over my Game Boy.

"I'm not sure I'm going to be able to sleep tonight," I said. I waited for her to look up from the game. Her thumbs worked the pink buttons furiously; she was trying to beat her record, which was the long number written on the yellow piece of paper taped to the coffee table beside her. I didn't play the Game Boy much but she played it all the time, even taking it to work with her to play during breaks; she was obsessed with Tetris, a game where small jagged bricks inch down the screen, and the point is to fit them back together. It was a game about making order out of chaos, putting back together what rained down in pieces.

"Why not?" she asked.

I tried to swallow the sharp lump wedged in my throat. "I'm too scared."

"Scared of what?" Her eyes flicked over the top her glasses just long enough to see me fidget in front of her. I wore an old T-shirt of my Dad's that hung past my boxer shorts.

"Scared of the aliens," I confessed.

She pushed a button and put the Game Boy down. "You do not need to be scared of aliens," she said. "They aren't real."

But she'd seen the same show, hadn't she? She heard the stories of the weird lights descending out of the sky on dark rural roads. She heard the Texas woman describe the cold metal instruments the aliens used to probe her body. She heard about the paralyzed people waking up under their abductors' stare. And most crucially, she saw the penciled sketches—how people who had never met all described the same alien face: menacing lightbulb-shaped heads with mirrored, insect eyes and thin coin slots for mouths. Just because the idea of alien abductions sounded unbelievable didn't mean I couldn't also accept them as real.

Sometimes I stood like a flamingo when I was nervous about something. I'd cross my arms over my chest, balance on one foot, and prop the other foot against the standing leg, in the notch above the knee. Then I'd tilt my head down on one side to avoid the eyes of the person I was talking to. As my mother returned to her game, I watched the reflection in her glasses of the bricks falling from the sky, and stood there like a flamingo, hoping she'd know what I needed without me having to ask.

The alien abduction show aired in October, a month into my seventh grade year, and only a few months after we'd moved into our new house during the summer. Our old house was much smaller, with all three bedrooms and both bathrooms huddled together. In the new one, my bedroom was the last door at the end of a long hallway, and especially on that alien night, it seemed as if I were teetering at the very edge of the house, alone. We'd moved to a brand-new subdivision where every house had just been built on cleared lots. None of the yards had trees, only half had grass. And behind our back yard, empty fields stretched for miles—perfect landing pads for UFOS.

The morning after watching the alien show, as both my mother and I yawned during breakfast—she couldn't sleep in her sleeping bag on my floor because I couldn't stop tossing in my loud, squeaking bed—I thought I could survive this awful fear as long as I was never alone again; every abductee had been alone when they were taken. Unless the aliens were equipped to abduct whole families at a time, or entire classrooms of seventh graders, which the show last night didn't go into, it seemed possible to protect myself by always being in the presence of people.

As soon as I arrived at school, I headed for the library like I did every morning before class. I walked the stacks of books, strolled from A to Z as my finger slid along the slick plastic spines. I could judge books by their covers, so I was looking for unexpected colors or fancy embossed letters, something new. There was a blue book that I'd always liked looking at though never enough to actually read, and I pulled it down to spread open the cover. The plastic protector cracked and hissed, the sound felt loud. The library was quiet of course, but suddenly it was too quiet, because there was no one else around. Usually that silence and order was exactly the opposite of the crowded hallways where locker doors slammed and kids jostled your shoulders. That silence had always been a comfort; but that day, to be hidden behind the tall shelves was certain danger.

I returned to the hall and meandered the maze of the building. I passed the boys who roamed in packs with their hands in pockets and the girls who stood in secretive groups and pointed at each other's skirts. My first class was Biology, and it wasn't until I sat down in my desk, the teacher shuffling papers behind hers, that I remembered what went on in there. Behind me, at tall black countertops, just a few weeks before, we had dissected frogs. In my mind, that's what the abduction was like: my cold body splayed in a metal baking pan and split open with sewing pins. Our poor frogs were stiff and rubbery, and their organs, once we peeled the skin back, were slippery and bloated. We poked them with our scalpels, identified a list of parts, and if one of us (me) was too squeamish to touch something like the gallbladder, our teacher stomped across the classroom, grabbed our tray, and pinched the little round organ with her naked fingers to prove it was that easy.

At school that year, even before my alien abduction fear arrived overnight, I sometimes felt as if I were a specimen like those dissected frogs. Seventh grade seemed like the year when we were all noticing each other's bodies. I'd overheard girls discussing boys' bodies, deciding who had the nicest-looking legs or arms, and once, in music class after careful deliberation with the two top contenders standing side by side, the best butt.

(I was so skinny, they told me, that I didn't even have one.) Of course the boys noticed bodies too: the girls. I watched their eyes as they moved over the females; sometimes I imagined that the girls could actually feel the boys' eyeballs skimming over their skin like a wet finger.

I settled into the easy pattern of teachers droning and bells ringing, and felt most comfortable in class. In the halls, the other seventh graders passed and nudged me out of their way, hollered over my head, which was business as usual. But still I wondered if my fear covered my skin like sunburn, the way it felt.

Then, at lunch, everywhere I looked in the cafeteria made me think of autopsies. All the gleaming trays of knives and forks lined up like medical implements, the pans of sickly-yellow noodles and brilliant red baked cherry crisp, conveyor belts and meat slicers. Because I couldn't go sit in the library like I normally did, I sat down at one end of a long table full of other seventh grade boys; I pretended I was one of them by laughing when they laughed—a strategy I'd been working on already. I'd gone to school with all of them since kindergarten, but that year, I was uneasy around them because they always talked about sex, which I dreaded because they all seemed to have much more experience than I did—which was none. In fact, it was a couple of weeks before, the last time the lunch ladies served that cherry crisp dessert, that one of them reached across the table and shoved his thumb into the steaming red stuff on my tray. He drew his hand back, licked his thumb, and announced to the table that he had just popped my cherry. "Now you can stop walking around like you've got something stuck up your ass," he said. Staring down at the hole torn out of my dessert, I sat frozen and unable to speak. The boys around me laughed.

After lunch was suddenly the worst hour of my whole day: fifth period, gym, when at the end of class, we were required to shower—to stand in an echoing, tiled room under nozzles that poked out of the wall. Like every other day that year, as much as I wanted to look at the other boys in the shower—I was noticing bodies too—I kept my eyes pointed to the floor. I knew looking was dangerous, though I couldn't help noticing the details of their bodies that made me want to hide mine. Armpit hair, long muscles in their legs, acne bumps on their shoulders, dark fuzz on their chins.

But that day, in the shower, I realized I really was a specimen worth examining because there was no one in that room who looked like me. In sixth grade, there had been three of us—the short boys shoved to the front row of group pictures and picked last for sports teams. But in seventh grade, I was the last of my kind with the smooth, small, white body. If aliens wanted to study humans, then I was so weird that they would have to abduct me. It seemed inevitable, guaranteed. They were going to take me onto their spaceship and pull me apart.

Several days passed. My mother slept in my room each night. As far as I knew, she didn't tell either my younger brother or father why I needed her in there. I'd asked her not to. I knew that thirteen was too old to act the way I was acting.

On Sunday night, after my brother and father had gone to their beds and most of the house was quiet and dark, I lay alone in my bedroom, and offered God a bargain; if I had to be abducted by aliens, if that was part of His plan, then would He please please let me sleep through the whole thing so I would never know the difference. I took it to God because without my mother saying so, I knew she and I had reached the end of her patience. In the way that she was avoiding bed-time by not taking her bath or changing into her nightgown at her usual time, I could tell she thought I should sleep alone again.

But the idea of going back to school the next day had undone me. Something about being surrounded by crowds of students, the heavy steel doors and the green-tiled halls. And as I lay in bed, dreading Monday morning, the gentle pops and ticks of the new house settling into its foundation weren't helping either. Every little noise nudged my skin with fear. Each one was the opening of a spaceship hatch or an alien's foot touching down on the roof above me. As I squeezed my eyes shut, wishing sleep would smother me, I thought about how my fear of aliens had become less important than what the fear had revealed—at school, even when I was with all the other kids, I was still always alone, and that solitude had something to do with my body.

I ripped off my blanket, skipped across the carpet to

my door, twisted the knob, and tiptoed fast down the long hallway—each silent step bringing me closer to the warm light of my mother's lamp. By then, she was in her spot in the living room, playing her game. It was 11 o'clock.

I stood in front of her, like I had four nights before, and waited for her to notice. The moment stretched out with the TV murmuring from the corner and her thumbs tapping the plastic buttons on the Game Boy. I knew she was thinking about me, stalling and trying to figure out what to do.

"What's wrong?" she said.

"I'm still scared. I still can't sleep."

"You know," she said, and then stopped, and I thought it was because the bricks were falling down her screen too quickly and she needed a second to catch up, so I said nothing. "You know," she started again, "if you don't get over this, we're going to have to take you somewhere. You're going to have to talk to somebody."

"Like who?" I asked.

"A doctor," she said. "A psychologist."

I slumped onto the loveseat across from her, and my bare legs disappeared under my T-shirt. I didn't even need my flamingo pose to pretend I was defeated. *A doctor, a psychologist.* Her words kept hitting my ears like a ringing phone that everyone thinks someone else will answer. There *was* something wrong with me, and it was more than just being scared. This wasn't the right way for a kid my age to act and we needed someone else to fix it. The doctors would probably split me open the same way the aliens wanted to, the long cut from under the chin straight down to the crotch that my Biology teacher showed us with the frogs.

"Honey, why are you scared?" she asked.

I wanted to tell her it was only a matter of time before I'd be abducted by aliens. There was something hidden in my body. That was why I looked so different. And why the other boys said I walked the way I did, and made fun of my voice. I wanted to tell her I tried to protect myself at school by making myself invisible, hoping to slink past everyone in the hall without being noticed. And how the trouble had arrived when I found out that the aliens were after me, when suddenly I needed those people I was trying to hide from to keep me safe. But it was too late. Who could notice an invisible boy was missing?

"I don't know," I said, my voice breaking into pieces. "Just don't make me sleep in there by myself." I didn't want to need her so much, not at my age, but that didn't mean I still didn't need her.

She kept playing her game, buttons clicking and clicking. I watched her, and waited. *One more night*. If she would sleep in my room once more, I could handle the next day. Or anyway I could pretend to, and I thought about how good I was getting at pretending. Staring at her so hard that my vision blurred, I waited for her answer. On the screen in front of her, I imagined the bricks falling faster and faster, and how at some point, she wouldn't be able to keep up. Which was the tough secret of that kind of game—the better you got at it, the harder it was.

If You Knew Then
What I Know Now

· · · · ·

In your sixth-grade social studies class, fourth hour, when Mrs. Perry assigns the group project on European World Capitals, don't look at Mark. Don't look at Jared. See if there's another group you can get into, the quiet girl who sits in front of you needs someone to work with too. If you could avoid working on this project with those two boys, you could avoid all of this.

If you do end up in a group with Mark and Jared, you should insist that you meet at the library. If you could meet at the library, then they couldn't do what they are planning to do. If you do agree to meet with them at Mark's house, then I don't know what to tell you. If you meet there, it's probably all going to happen the way it's going to happen.

You will show up at Mark's. His sister will answer the door. Your backpack will weigh down on your back, and his Dad will be watching football in the living room but you don't see him, you only hear the dull roar of the TV crowd. His sister will point you down the hallway. "First room on the right," she will say, "across from the bathroom." You'll knock on the closed door.

You'll think it's odd that the door is closed. They know you're coming over. They know it's the day before the project is due. They know all of this. You will hear whispering on the other side of door, and then it's swung open and Mark stands there, smiling. Jared is flung across the bed reading a magazine. The television glows in the corner. A video game is on, but the action is paused, a figure with winged shoes and a bow and arrow frozen in the middle of the arc of his jump. You've played this game before. You're good at it.

You'll let your backpack slump to the floor, unzip it, and pull out your books. You'll balance them in your lap, split open folders and pull out the assignment worksheet. "OK," you will say. You read over the assignment, the social studies project you're supposed to be working on, and you won't notice that they aren't listening to you. You won't notice they are mouthing words to each other. You won't know their plan is about to take shape.

And you won't know when they ask you to grab the box of Hostess cupcakes on the kitchen counter that they really don't care about the cupcakes. They just need you out of the room for a second. Of course you'll do it. You'll hop up and head to the kitchen. You're so excited to be over at Mark's house, hanging out with other boys. It's what your mother has been telling you to do for years: "You need to spend more time with boys. You should do more things that boys like to do. Why are you always just hanging around girls?" That's why what you see when you walk back in the room will be so confusing. You'll think, "This isn't what boys do, this isn't what I thought we were supposed to do."

The door will be shut when you return from the kitchen, though you'll know you certainly didn't shut it as you left. The rest of the house will be quiet, though you can still hear the football game from the living room. You will twist the knob and push open the door, and you will see them, on the bed. Jared will be under Mark, and they are turned so you can't see their faces, not the front of their faces anyway, and they are pretending to kiss. Mark's thick forearms will be stiffly curled around Jared, Jared's glasses will be folded, shoved in the corner of the windowsill. Both of them will peek under not-quite-closed eyelids. You will know right off they aren't really kissing because one of them—it's hard to tell if it's Mark or if it's Jared—will slide a flat palm in between their wet mouths so their lips can't touch. But they hope you will think they are kissing and that's the idea behind this. You will know they aren't kissing, but you will also know they want to pretend they are kissing. You will guess correctly when you think the project isn't going to be worked on today.

They will pull away after you've stood there for a second. You will start to step back, though you don't really know where to go, and they will say, "come back, come back in, we're sorry." You are back in the room, and they are sitting on Mark's navy-blue comforter holding hands. You'll feel immediately nervous, your face will feel suddenly hot and pink. There's no way now for you to cover your skin for them not to see the blushing color and for them not to see how you try to swallow, though your throat is too dry.

They will start talking about it, which you were afraid they would do. "What's wrong?" Jared will ask you. Mark will ask, "Yeah, what's wrong, Ryan?" They will look at each other and down at their hands, one flopped over the other. "We hope you don't mind us doing this stuff. This is just something we do," Jared says, and he will shrug as if it's normal, as normal as note passing. "Don't you ever do stuff like this, Ryan?" Mark will ask you, and here you are, at the point of all this. "You like to kiss guys, right, Ryan?" They are trying to get you to say things about yourself that you won't be ready to say for several more years and that's what will hurt the most about this afternoon. Hurt more than never hanging out with Mark or Jared again. Hurt more than anything anybody will say at school about what actually happened in Mark's bedroom. It will hurt most when you realize they saw something in you that you thought you'd hidden so well you couldn't even see it yourself anymore. They found something in you before you did. They saw it and there it will be, holding a box of cupcakes.

Years after, you will wonder how you managed to get through the rest of junior high and high school without ever speaking to Mark or Jared again, but somehow you will do it. In high school Jared will trade his brown glasses for contacts, and you will overhear girls in hallways whispering to each other about how pretty his eyes are. Mark will begin hanging out with the boys who wear dark jackets throughout the whole school year, no matter the weather, the boys who smoke in the sunken garden behind the school building, sitting on rotted railroad ties, sharing cigarettes every morning before the bell rings and after lunch. You will eventually find your own friends, and from that afternoon in sixth grade to the evening of your high school graduation you will never tell another person about Mark and Jared's kiss.

One day someone will ask you about the first time you kissed a boy, and you will think of this kiss, the one between Mark and Jared, the kiss that isn't really a kiss and isn't really yours. You could almost laugh. It will be funny to you, in a way, how important this kiss will be—it was the first kiss between two men, however young they were, you will have seen. Funny how of all the kisses in your life this is the one you will think most about. It will be the biggest kiss you ever saw.

Before you will ever be able to actually tell another person about this kiss, you will try to write it as fiction. You will try to recast it as a short story. You will have moved to Chicago by then, after college and college creative writing classes, and you will spend evenings sitting in cafés, working, bent over a legal pad, and one night, this kiss will come to you, and you will think, "now that's a good story." You will begin by vividly describing it, the class project and the bedroom door and the glasses on the windowsill. There will be something about watching it happen on the page, about having control over the afternoon and these three boys. You will try to rename them, but you will never find the perfect substitutes for the names *Mark* or *Jared*. Without *Mark* or *Jared* the story somehow won't work. You will read over it, you will witness the afternoon again, and it won't seem real. You will try to change the layout of Mark's house, change the ages of the boys, move them through time, make them years older or younger. The boy in the story holding the cupcakes—even in the fictional version, you include the cupcakes—just standing there, blushing, his stunned silence, is something you yourself can't believe. You will think this doesn't seem real, it doesn't sound like something that would really happen.

Finally, you decide to just tell it. It will be almost eleven years from that sixth-grade afternoon. You will sit with three close friends and together drink several bottles of wine. None of them will have gone to your high school and none of them will have heard of Mark or Jared. You will sit in an old armchair, a plastic cup hanging from your hand. Votive candles will be scattered on a coffee table, their dull lights reflecting across the bare hardwood floor in the dim apartment. When you begin to tell the story you will feel the rise of a familiar panic. There will be the dry throat and the same flushed and sweating neck. Your friends will watch your face turn. And it will feel silly, your body still affected, still intimidated. A man in his twenties afraid of two twelve-year-old boys on a bed, miles away and years gone.

If you can't stop any of this, if you can wait sixteen years, it will end well, or at least, better than you'd guess. At your ten-year high-school reunion, near the night's end, on the crowded patio, Jared will approach you.

At the reunion, throughout the evening, you will have noticed that most of the boys from your high school—the football players and basketball players, the class officers and the prom king—are quickly balding or already bald, and somehow all shorter. Everyone's life is sort of rearranged: the quarterback walks on prosthetic feet now, and the class president is a Dallas Cowboys Cheerleader. You are taller than you were then and your classmates look at you and look again and tell you that you seem grown-up. And instead of hiding a part of yourself from them like you did in school you will have decided to bring your boyfriend.

You stand next to him. The open-bar is closed. Classmates make plans to meet at nearby bars, promise to e-mail each other, send letters, and exchange photos of children to keep in touch. Your best friend and your boyfriend are smoking cigarettes. You are standing outside with them on a patio overlooking a courtyard, waiting to walk back to your hotel room and look through the senior yearbook you brought, to point at pictures and talk about the faces. Out of the clump of classmates and spouses Jared suddenly walks up to you. You already knew he was at the reunion, and you almost thought you'd made it through the night without talking to him. He looks like he did in high school—big and thick, a round chest, thick stump legs, a spread-out face with large, wet eyes—only he's losing his hair and his skin is lined with age. He has a wife; she's extremely thin. Jared extends his hand, and you shake it. He says "Hey, Ryan," like he's surprised to see you. The patio is very dark. Classmates crowd around you both, squeezing the space away, their faces covered in shadows. Jared's nametag—like your nametag, with a scan of your senior picture printed on it—is stuck to his shirt, a crease down its center and dotted by drops of beer.

Your boyfriend and your best friend drop away, leaning to each other in their own conversation; they won't notice Jared. He asks you the customary questions, the ones answered this evening already a hundred times. Where do you live now, how are you doing, what are you doing, do you like Chicago? You tell him, wondering why he's talking to you. You are still afraid of Jared. Or at least you are still afraid of that Jared, the one with the glasses on an afternoon in sixth grade. The conversation comes to an end, once you've exhausted the usual, casual exchange. Then Jared lifts his big arm to your shoulder. He says: "Hey, listen, you probably won't even remember what I am talking about, but there was this time, at fuckin' Mark's house, when—" and you stop him.

"I know what you're going to say."

"You do?"

"I know exactly what you're going to say." You are surprised, too.

"I don't have to say it?"

"No," you say, and actually you don't want him to say it, you don't want to hear him tell it. It would seem too easy, too obvious for this tormentor to apologize at your reunion. You wouldn't even test this moment on the page—if it were a story you could write—since no reader would believe it. "It couldn't really happen this way," you think, standing in front of Jared, watching it happen.

"Well, look, I just want to say that what we did, it was stupid. I'm really sorry. We were just asshole kids."

You think it's strange that you assumed you were the only boy hurt by that kiss in Mark's bedroom. But you see that Jared carries that day with him like you do; he carries a shame not very different from yours. Somehow you've shared a scar this many years. You say to Jared that just knowing he remembers that afternoon is enough. He thanks you and grabs you again. On your shoulder his hand feels a little like the warmth of comfort, and a little like the squeeze of danger.

Youth Group

· · · · ·

I'm sleeping against the van window when they all start gasping at the sight of the Rockies and wake me up. I squint in the sudden bright afternoon, looking for these mountains, but all I can see is a distant dark bulk. I'm in the last row of seats, crammed against the side of the passenger van because I'm sitting next to Aaron. He's sprawled out like always, legs and giant sneakers spread across our row. And I know sitting anywhere else would be more comfortable but I always sit next to Aaron. In fact, I *have* to sit next to him because I'm in love with him. Though none of us has figured that out yet.

I'm fourteen years old and there are twelve of us in the van—besides Aaron and me, seven other high school kids and three adult chaperones. This is our church youth group summer trip, and we've almost made it from Missouri to the campsite in Colorado where we'll stay the week. I'm yawning as Aaron notices my nap is finished, and then punches my shoulder. The hit makes my arm feel dead for a few seconds until the throbbing begins— my pulse flaring right where a bruise will emerge tomorrow. "Mountains," he says, pointing to the front of the van.

"Thank you so much." I say it deadpan and rub my arm.

Aaron is a year older than me. He's tall and solid, a sophomore player on our school's varsity football team. He's going to be in the Army so he's always wearing camouflage. The sun reaching into the van lights up the clear bristly hair that covers his chin, arms and legs. He smiles and scratches his shin near the spot where a spider almost killed him. A rare pleasure of mine is asking him to stab this spider scar with a knife; the tissue is so damaged and desiccated that even a blade can't split it open. It's his invincible spot, as though he's Achilles in reverse. I love the story of the spider bite and when I've heard it and watched him press a knife into the scar, I've imagined his hospital stay, the deadly fevers, a doctor's needle squirting antidote into his veins at the very last second. That Aaron, the weak, helpless one is so different from this one next to me, it's almost as if part of him did die from the spider's bite, leaving an Aaron I can marvel at, and be a little afraid of.

"Here," Gina says from the seat in front of us, handing me her paperback book. "I'm done with chapter six." We're sharing the same novel because I didn't bring one. She reads a couple of chapters, then I catch up. It's a book about married geneticists— the husband is sterile so he and his wife create a test tube baby who mutates into an amazingly intelligent but psychotic toddler; the kid ages too quickly though and eventually tries to murder them. Sex *and* violence. It's the best book I've ever read.

I say thanks, and fan out the pages to find my chapter.

Gina is the oldest of us. She'll be a senior in high school this fall. Whenever I'm with her, I somehow feel younger than I actually am. She turns around in her seat and rests her chin on the back of it. "Aaron, come here," she says. He leans his ear close to her mouth, she whispers something, and then he cups his hand around his mouth and whispers something back to her. I watch and strain to hear their secret but everyone is still talking about the stupid mountains. Almost touching her dark straight hair, Aaron's large hand is tightly strung with fleshy wires and knobs; the tiny twitches moving under his skin remind me of a machine, of what I see when I peek under the cover of my piano at home while I'm pressing on the keys.

Miles go by. The nearest huge mountain slowly rises above our van and glares down like a bully. I've tried ignoring their secret but can't. Silently, I elbow Aaron, point to Gina's back and mouth *What?* He shrugs and says loudly, "Just a question from your book. Mind your own business." Gina turns around. She eyes him, then looks at me, looks at him again, and this time, she smiles. He licks his fingertips and wipes them on my face.

The campsite, for church groups and Christian families, is called "Sermon on the Mount," and it features huge vinyl tents that look like white hay bales, a cafeteria and fellowship center, showers and indoor toilets, picnic tables and a swimming pool. The boys are in one tent with the male chaperones, and the girls are next-door. I follow Aaron, the other boys in our group, and our youth leader into the tent where we flump our sleeping bags into a heap on the floor.

After that, all of us stand in the shade between the tents trading dazed expressions. Brad, one of the other boys, sneaks behind Aaron and tries to clamp him in a headlock. Aaron easily tosses him off and then presses him down into some gravel and pine needles. Brad begs for mercy, then mutters he'll get even later. When our youth group goes on trips like this, whether we stay in tents, cabins or hotel rooms, the boys organize epic pillow fights. Sometimes I think pillow fighting is the real reason Aaron is in youth group. He's impossible to knock down and he's strong enough to land his feather pillow on your cheek like a sack of flour. He delivers instant headaches with a single tooth-loosening blow. In previous summers when we've spent weeks at a camp with cabins in the Missouri woods, each night, the bunk beds were stripped and the mattresses were all piled in the middle of the room. All of the boys would sock each other until only one was left standing: Aaron, on the uneven mass of mattresses, the boys with weaker arms and fluffier pillows whimpering at his feet.

Because I weigh about 90 pounds, I'm a watcher of pillow fights instead of an actual fighter—although I am usually pulled into the ring at least once, most often when Aaron grips my ankles and yanks me in for a pummeling. I'm the whipping boy of youth group. It's just so easy for them to hold me upside down or wad me up and shove me in a kitchen cupboard. And, like the bruise that's rising up on my arm from Aaron's punch in the van, there is some pain. But as much as I make a big show when they wring my arms with Indian sunburns or twist wet fingers in my ears, as much as I squeal in protest and flail around, silently and secretly, I do crave the attention—especially Aaron's.

He lets go of Brad just as our guides tromp up the gravel path. Blake and Cindy, fit and muscled, blonde and pink-cheeked, both wearing gold crosses on chains and expensive sunglasses. Their smiles are identical. This week they'll take us white water rafting, rock climbing, rappelling and even hiking—several miles out where we'll pitch tents on a mountain, cook over a fire and drink from a perfectly clear stream. Blake sweeps his arm across the wide sky and points to a short mountain on the other side of the interstate. A glacier slid down its face and dug out the straight scar we see now. Then, a road was cut across the mountain, clearing out a line of pines about two-thirds of the way up. With my eyes, I follow his tanned arm drawing a cross in the air and then I see it carved there into the mountain. "God's mark on God's mountain," he says. Blake tells our circle to join hands for prayer before dinner. I knew this was coming so I'm already standing next to Aaron though I pretend some reluctance, putting on my *Can you believe this guy?* look.

Church is just like school—we go because we have to. The worst part is waking up early on Sundays and getting dressed up. Once we get to church, and slide down a pew to sit in the sanctuary, I'm fine because I only have to pretend to listen. I'm free to daydream, to make up stories in my head. As long as I keep my eyes pointed up front, nobody knows how I'm not really getting it when the pastor says *salvation, grace* or *sin*—words that sound important but don't mean much. I imagine that for everybody else those words have a physical sensation, a feeling like your belly is full of warm water or the lightheadedness after spinning in one spot over and over, and because I never feel anything in church or when I pray, I assume I must be doing it wrong. Like now, holding Aaron's hand in the circle of kids, the only thing I feel is his hand. Blake says, "Amen."

Time to eat. As Blake and Cindy lead the group to the cafeteria, I try matching Aaron's huge stride. A few paces ahead of us, Gina turns to another girl, points at Blake's tiny blue shorts, and whispers, "He's hot."

The next day, we cram ourselves into wetsuits and go rafting on the Arkansas River. There's a guide in each raft to steer our inflatable vessel with long wooden oars, point out rock formations and tell us when to bail the inches of water pooling at our feet. Almost every stretch of the river has a name— Gunbarrel Rush, the Widowmaker, Sledgehammer Falls, Big Drop. For six hours, the water jerks us down its course and I can't stop thinking how easily my face could be scoured off by each jutting boulder we pass. My wetsuit is three sizes too big, and between dangerous spots on the river, I concentrate on trying to flatten the spongy wrinkles around my middle and crotch. Aaron looks like a superhero in his wetsuit—as dark, hulking and polished as Batman.

When we return to camp that evening, we're all sunburnt and soggy. After I wrench off my wetsuit in a bathroom stall, and change into a T-shirt and shorts, I limp into the big tent and collapse on my sleeping bag. With the late afternoon sun slanting over the mountains, the air is warm and still, and after the daylong turbulence, I don't mind it. One by one, the others climb into the tent, including Aaron, to change clothes and rest before dinner.

His army duffel bag is unzipped next to me. I nod to him as he unlaces his sneakers and brushes sand grit off his feet and shins. I'm lying on my back, my damp hair grinding into my pillow, and I throw my right arm over my face like it's too bright. In the blurry margin of my vision, I see Aaron lift his chin and pull down the zipper of the wetsuit at the root of his neck. The teeth unlock in a long high note like a sigh, and from the noise and movement beside me, I know he's stripped off the suit, and he's down to his camouflage trunks. He steps out of the suit and flings it into a wriggling pile near my feet; drops of water hit my petrified legs. More digging in the duffel bag, then a T-shirt is unfolded and shaken out, snapping like a flag.

My eyes still point at the crossbars holding up the tent's ceiling but they want to peek at Aaron. I want to see him, the hidden parts of his body I've tried so hard never to think about. If I turned my head just a bit, if I only glanced, I could probably catch a quick flash and he wouldn't notice. And if he did notice, couldn't I pass it off as just looking around? My tired eyes wandering without *really* looking? Would it have to mean something?

There's the sudden soft shushing of his swimming trunks as he pushes them down his legs. Now, he's naked beside me, no more than a few feet away. Right there. I'm frozen, afraid of what I want to see, afraid of what I want to do, afraid of what he'll do if I look. In my head, with my eyes staring hard at the black X above me, I try picturing what he looks like, and I can see all the parts of Aaron I've already seen, with a murky grey nothing floating over the rest.

In a few seconds, he's pulled on fresh clothes, it's over. He drops his heavy body to the platform to put on socks and shoes. With his right leg, the spider leg, he reaches over and rubs his bare foot on my face.

"You going to dinner or what?" he says.

"Knock it off," I say, pushing him off, pretending to be crabby.

We're ready early in the morning for the hike—through a forest and up a mountain to an expanse of grass where we'll spend the night. Blake warns us how tough it's going to be. "It's June," he says. "And today, you're going to touch snow. That's how far we're going." I'm not impressed, I can see the snow from here.

We're all strapped down under enormous backpacks, full of gear we have to carry though most of it isn't actually ours. Because I'm so short, my pack stretches over my head and something rough rubs my neck left then right then left again as I waddle under its weight. "You all right?" Aaron asks.

"Oh yeah."

The hike takes all day, and there are several moments when the cramp in my side almost forces me to toss my body down the scrubby flank of the mountain. At one point, Blake doubles back to encourage me; I'm the last of the group, behind all the girls, which isn't necessarily surprising to me but is strange to him. Plus I've already drunk all the water in my canteen. We've gone about a quarter of a mile.

"Hey, big guy," he says. "You've got to pick it up if we want to reach the peak by dark."

I want to say something but I've lost the ability so I just nod and squeeze my cramp and continue daydreaming that I'm not really there.

When we reach the grassy flatness that will be our campsite, we pitch our tents and then gather in a circle around Blake as he bows his head and thanks God for our safe journey and for this majesty. But the view is so gorgeous it's fake, as if we're standing in front of giant postcards. Wide sky, thick pines, the snowy peak reaching up and sparkling, an actual babbling brook—I recognize the beauty but that doesn't mean I feel anything. With Blake's hushed voice praying, his words droning like a hum, I can't keep my eyes on anything besides Aaron's sweaty forearms. And when I look, there is real feeling—something physical that runs through me with a sudden thrill like fear.

At the moment, I don't know what staring at Aaron really means. I've tricked myself into thinking that I like looking at his body because mine is so small and shapeless, as if this is Mrs. Kline's second-hour biology class and Aaron is one of the rubbery frog specimens we have to examine and touch and report on precisely. At the moment, I've also never kissed anyone and don't really understand what kissing is, or what you do with your body once you start kissing someone. So I don't think about that either when I stare at him. I don't think about what his body could do to mine. What I do think about is all the strength working inside him, the force when he collides with players on the football field, how this hike was nothing for him, not even hard. And sometimes I do wonder what it would be like to take on that force, to be crushed by him and squeezed from the inside out—like the cramp in my side except over my whole body.

After the prayer, Blake says it's time to keep hiking to that snowy peak, and he points to it looming above the trees. General excitement among the group—the tying of shoes, the chewing of GORP, the rubbing of sunscreen on noses. I nudge Aaron's arm. "He really thinks we want to hike again?" I ask, smirking.

"I'm going," he says. "But you probably don't have to go if

you don't want to." He rolls his sleeves over the humps of each shoulder.

"Aaron," Gina shouts. She's standing with Blake. She says, "Let's go," and he heads after her.

For a second or two I consider following him, but decide to throw myself across a boulder, to just lie in the sun and pout instead.

An hour later, I shake out of a daze when I hear distant laughter, screams. I open my eyes and squint at the mountain peak. They made it. The group stands at the edge of the snow, straddling the line between white and green, cupping out snowballs, propping their flat hands over their eyes to look at everything below. Blake points at things. They nod. And then I see Aaron, charging through the snow in his shorts, Gina on him, piggyback. Her arms are locked around his neck, they're both squealing and laughing in the sun.

That night, after the campfire dinner, after tiptoeing in the crickety darkness to pee, I sleep in a small three-person tent with Aaron and Brad. Between Aaron and Brad. They each unroll their sleeping bags along the tent's sides so I'm in the middle. Which is scarier than white water rafting, scarier even than hanging from my fingertips off the smooth face of a rock when we went climbing. Because it's exactly what I wanted and now I don't want it. I'm scared most of the defenselessness of sleep, of this pull towards Aaron forcing me to reach out to him in the night or say something weird in a dream. As we settle down on the tent floor, bodies stuffed and sweating against the flannel linings of sleeping bags, I lie stiff and pray that I won't accidentally touch Aaron.

With the steady wind outside rippling the fabric walls, and Aaron and Brad breathing low and slow on either side of me, I feel like I'm sealed inside a lung. Lying on my side, I can't stop listening to the eerie quiet, all the sounds I don't normally notice, like my heartbeat tapping on my eardrums or my eyelashes scraping my pillow as I blink in the dark. But then I have to flip over so I'm on my back; I can't sleep facing him because what if he wakes up? What if these feelings are visible on my face like pillowmarks? As I wriggle around, my shoulder brushes his but he doesn't stir.

So there are only inches between us. Our shoulders—mine white and thin with the dark smudge of a new bruise, his firm and knotted. I imagine my shoulder reaching out like a fingertip to touch his, just pressing against it and staying there. Listening to the mountain, I fall asleep pushing my finger against my bruise, and each time there's comfort in the certainty of the pain.

We return to "Sermon on the Mount" the next day, our last before going home. We wander around with zombie faces, all of us dazzled by the exhaustion of walking up and down mountains. It's the part of the trip where we're getting sick of each other—when I can guess what someone will say before they say it. Even Aaron starts bugging me. Something about how he won't stay in one spot and how I keep losing track of him.

Later on, we say good night to the adults and hang out in the swimming pool under the too-bright stars with the mountains huddled around us. I'm wearing my T-shirt in the water. We splash each other. When that gets boring, we try some stunts—Brad attempts some tricky dives, cannonballs, belly flops. Gina suggests trying to stand and balance on Aaron's shoulders. And of course, she goes first. He hoists her up and grips her ankles as she wiggles with her arms straight out to either side. Pitching back, she collapses into the pool and comes up spurting water and laughing. They try again and again, and she keeps falling.

"Let Ryan try," someone says. Maybe it will be easier for Aaron to hoist me, instead of her. I *am* the smallest one. In slow motion through the water, I walk to him, and he crouches down, neck-deep in the pool. I steady myself with my hands on his slippery back and then press my feet into the rubbery divots of muscle in his shoulders. He counts, one two three, and then pushes us up and out of the water. Once he's braced, I stand too, balancing perfectly.

As we stand above the water, I fight the urge to pull on my clinging T-shirt. My shirtsleeve is hiked up, I know that Aaron's bruise is probably showing, I don't want anyone to see it— they're all looking up at us with hushed faces. But to fix it might set us off-balance, might force me to wiggle too much and fall, splayed onto Aaron. Everything sits still for several seconds. But before I can move, Aaron tips himself forward while holding my feet, and his weight pulls me toward the pool.

We crash into the surface. I twist under the water, and his hands surround my shoulders and push down. I can't open my eyes because I can't stand the chlorine so there's only the dark and the swoosh of legs thrashing and bubbles tickling my face. My arms stretch out for something, and as Aaron holds me under, one of my hands presses full against the warmth of his chest while the other wraps around his hard arm. His body feels like the slick stones we lifted from the river when we rafted. I brace myself against him and we float for a second or two with me feeling the sensation of feeling him. Suddenly he wrenches me up, back to the air. When I open my eyes, he's several feet ahead, swimming away.

He joins the rest of them in the shallow end, sitting on the stairs submerged at the entrance of the pool. I swim to them too, and we lounge in the warm water under the floodlights on telephone poles, while hunched over in the distance the outline of the mountains is almost as dark as the sky. Everyone is talking about penises.

Gina can't imagine what it's like to have one, so she's asking. What does it feel like to be kicked there? In the morning, why do guys always wake up with erections? Aaron and Brad, and the other boys laugh and joke and answer. Gina's swimsuit is yellow and black plaid, and it looks like it doesn't fit her, as if it's too tight around her breasts, which she covers by crossing her arms in front of them. I'm staying quiet, grinning and smirking according to how the other boys react to Gina. She stands with her back against the turquoise tiles of the pool wall, stroking her fingers across the top of the water; the other girls beside her are quiet too, and continuously shifting—adjusting swimsuit straps, fixing ponytails.

What about sex, she asks. "Why do some guys finish before you even get started?" she says, coyly. This silences the other boys. Brad says, "Oh my God," and Aaron says, "Wow." Gina smiles again. "I'm just asking. I'm just asking. Why can't I ask that question?"

Brad starts to answer. Then blushes. Then continues and gets embarrassed again. Aaron takes over. "Sometime you're just too, you know, excited? You just can't stop." His shoulders shrug. His big beautiful wet shoulders.

"What are blue balls?" Gina asks. "They don't really turn blue, do they?"

"No," Aaron snorts.

"So what are they then?" she presses.

"They just hurt," he says, his eyes focusing on hers, as though they're opponents in a staring contest. "You get them when you're hard for a long time without—"

"Oh," she says. "So what hurts?"

"Your *balls*," Aaron says, grinning again.

"But why does it hurt?" she asks, skeptically.

I decide to answer this one. "It just hurts because you're excited, and then it's over, and you're like 'okay, what now?'" I stand with my arms up, palms to the sky, in the cartoon pose of a question. I know the answer because I remember it from health class. It's something about blood flow—who doesn't know that? Everyone in the pool nods, waiting for the next question. Gina quickly turns to face me.

"And how would *you* know?" she says. Her forehead crinkles in disbelief, and she shakes her head and snickers. I feel a sting in her look and her words—how she knows I've never had sex because she knows why. Brad starts laughing, and he flicks his hand against the water and splashes me. The girls laugh, and the other boys laugh, and then Aaron laughs. I stand there, heat rushing up and drying out my mouth as if I'm on the mountain hike again.

Because I thought we were all just pretending; I didn't think any of the kids in the pool had actually had sex. In youth group, we talk about waiting for marriage, about love and men and women, and most often, about temptation. And because I never feel tempted by girls, I assume not giving in is easy for everybody else. I don't know yet that my desires live inside a tiny spot too tough to open. In the pool, under the white lights, even though my face is pink, I laugh too. I splash Brad back and keep laughing because I want it all to be a joke.

———

Somehow, since the last time we drove over it a week ago, Kansas has stretched out three or four times its actual size. In my seat, my body begins to feel stunted, like I'm compressing myself by being stuck in here. The sun shines in on our faces and arms but our legs are freezing from the full-blast AC. I'm sitting next to Aaron who is sitting next to Gina. A long flannel blanket that's covered in potato chip crumbs is pulled over all three of us.

Gina finishes our novel. "Here," she says, reaching over Aaron and thrusting it into my hands. "The ending is stupid. You don't have to read it if you don't want to." Thanks, I say, and flip to the third-to-last chapter where I left off. I don't see how it could end badly when everything that's come before has been so good. Aaron is sleeping, mouth wide open, and now Gina yanks on the blanket to cover her chest and arms and she tilts her head back and closes her eyes too.

The bump bump bump of the tires on the highway, the whine of the stereo, the soft murmur of conversations. I try to stay focused on the killer test-tube toddler, but I can't stop yawning and my eyes close suddenly, like the darkness is something I need. Quickly, I enter a dream. In an hour, I wake up when someone shouts that we're about to cross from Kansas into Missouri. I bend my stiff neck, pop my knuckles and look around in the sun-flooded van. Aaron still sits beside me, now staring at the road ahead of us like he's got to know exactly where he's going. I'm lucky enough to have skipped about 80 flat Kansas miles and I stretch, smiling as I yawn again.

What I've also skipped, what I won't know until about a year later, is what happened under the blanket while I was sleeping. I'll be in our high school's library with my English class, all of us supposed to be researching our term papers. Mine is on whale poaching. And because my teacher is down the hall smoking in the janitor's closet, when I see Aaron for the first time in a long time, he'll sit down at my table. It will be a long time because neither of us will go to youth group anymore. We'll talk in whispers about what's been going on and then we'll talk about this trip. And he'll tell me that when I slept beside him in the van, Gina pretended to sleep too, but crept her hand under the blanket and slid it into his shorts. And the night before, the night all of us stood in the swimming pool and talked about blue balls, after everyone else went to sleep, Aaron and Gina had sex. And as he leans in close to whisper the details—how they searched for a wide enough shadow, how she laid her beach towel over gravel and pulled him down—I'll finally understand I feel something real for Aaron, some kind of love, because I'll feel betrayed. But I'll confuse the feeling with disappointment, thinking they shouldn't have given into temptation, not during youth group, not at a religious campsite, not ever, because they didn't even like each other, not really, but most of all, because it's a *sin*, a word that also finally feels real. And I'll hate Gina for it, for making him do it, and for what she said in the pool, confusing that feeling too because it won't be hatred I feel for her—it will be jealousy.

Before we left Colorado to drive home, I decided to start collecting rocks. It seemed like something I should want to do, especially with so many rocks around, and I was immediately thrilled by my new hobby. I couldn't find anybody to walk around with so I set off alone, searching the campsite for something worth keeping forever. I didn't know exactly what kind of rock I was looking for—craggy, fossilized, smooth, or the kind where shapes emerge if you stare long enough and then suddenly recognize a lumpy apple, a man's fist, a curled fish. Near the bottom of the slope that reached up to the interstate, I found one. About as big as my head, this rock must've weighed nearly ten pounds. I had trouble holding it with one hand, but as I turned it in the sun, and looked at its weird streaks of rust and yellow and glittery black, I somehow knew this was what I wanted. Even wrapped up in T-shirts, the rock felt no less heavy, and I was barely able to heave my duffel bag into the van when it was time to go.

Now, barefoot on our church parking lot in Missouri, I stand at the back of the van with the rest of the group. The thought of leaving them, all of us going to separate houses and families is awful; I've been sick of everybody but now I want to know what they're doing tonight. Aaron stands at the van doors and starts pulling apart the great mass of our luggage. He grips each suitcase from the pile, and swings it down to its weary owner. Mine's on the bottom. I watch him and know it will be days before I'll see him again—probably not until youth group next week. When he finally hands me my bag, and the weight of it tugs at my arm, I don't believe how much I struggle to carry something he doesn't even notice.

Cherry Bars

· · · · ·

We have to hear that one again. Angie sits up and presses the rewind button to stop the tape in exactly the right place, in the silence between the two songs. We're lying on a blanket in the park, eating the cherry bars my grandma baked this afternoon and singing along to the whine of Simon and Garfunkel on my battery-operated tape player. It's summer 1992, we're seventeen. A heavy tree stretches over us, leaves so dense most of the sunlight is blotted out and can't reach our blanket. We look like we've been flung, arms and legs bent and slapped down in odd directions. The cherry bars are thick and warm, red blobs swirling across the top. We pick chunks of them out of the blue plastic container my grandma made me promise to bring home. "Like I'm really going to throw it away," I muttered in Angie's car, as she reversed out of my driveway. My parents are on vacation so my grandma is staying with my brother and me, even though I'm old enough to watch us.

Angie and I are best friends. We are the precise age for believing that always living in the same town and seeing each other every day for the rest of our lives is possible. We'll always be best friends and never anything more. I know what happens when you date your best friend because that's what happened with Claire, who, before Angie, was my best friend until she was my girlfriend, then my ex-girlfriend, and now she's nothing. This won't happen with Angie, though, because I'm certain that we are forever.

"These cherry bars taste sweaty," I say. I'm sucking the sticky bits off my fingers. We're listening to the lyrics of "The Sound of Silence," trying to figure out a meaning no one else has ever found. This song means more to us than it did to them, and by "them," we mean the people who were around thirty years ago when this album was originally recorded, specifically our parents. We were born in the wrong time. Angie tie-dyes T-shirts in her back yard, and I wear round sunglasses like John Lennon. We relive these memories even though they aren't ours because our parents had hippies and protests and pot and JFK and Vietnam and what do we have: nothing.

Angie is beautiful. Her eyes are pale watery green. She says they are the same color as her birthstone, peridot, which I know is pronounced "pair-a-doe" but I say "pair-a-dot" just to be corrected. When we see each other in the narrow hallways at school in the morning, we say, "How are you the smorning?" and laugh, because some people actually say it that way. Angie's breasts are the largest I have ever seen in real life. She hates them. She lies on the blanket in the shade ripping up grass, letting it sift through her fingers. Her cotton T-shirt is striped yellow, and she's pulling at it, yanking the bottom cuff down over her waist and the V-neck up, to cover her cleavage. We have a secret hand signal when we are in public and her cleavage is showing. I do the signal—lightly stroke my own neck with thumb and forefinger—and she fixes her shirt.

I'm wearing shorts, Birkenstock sandals and a double XL T-shirt, even though I weigh approximately 100 pounds. I am the smallest boy in our class. My auburn hair is stiff from gel and hairspray and perfectly parted, a white straight line always cut across my head. It's hot today; the sun glaring down on the grass heats up its sharp smell, which makes me sneeze. I have a handful of wet tissues in my pocket. I wipe my nose with the worn shreds and stuff them back in my shorts. Angie rewinds the Simon and Garfunkel tape again. I have to hear this one part. It's from "Bookends" which is our song now. It used to be "America," where he and Kathy ride the bus and count the cars on the New Jersey Turnpike. Paul Simon and Art Garfunkel and Angie and me all sing, "Time it was and what a time it was, it was." We love that line—the reminiscence but also the wisdom we think we understand. We smile and fall down again on the blanket.

We start talking about Kevin, her ex-boyfriend and Claire, my ex-girlfriend. Angie and Kevin dated for 2 years. They had sex. Claire and I dated for a year and a half. We never kissed. Right now, Kevin and Claire are hanging out together, we just know it. We think Claire likes Kevin, and we don't like that at all.

———

Claire and I got to know each other when we were both actors in an experimental school play. We wore black turtleneck sweaters and stood in front of giant neon arrows while delivering monologues about teen issues. Our friendship deepened after rehearsals when I needed rides home—we performed the radio songs in her car and soon discovered we enjoyed melancholy music, melodrama and each other. We were also both writers and we already knew that one day we were going to be famous— she for her poetry, me for bestselling suspense thrillers about lawyers—and we constantly tried to impress each other with our words.

It wasn't long before Claire and I were best friends. When she ate dinner at my house, we whispered jokes and sayings my parents didn't understand. My mom would ask, "What?" and we'd smile or laugh at her, one of us nudging the other's shin under the table, my dad rolling his eyes. We made mixed tapes for each other, the music always organized in a theme. She made *Solitude* for me, a collection of moody, depressing songs with an illustrated booklet folded out of gray résumé paper. And we wrote notes, a lot of them. Both of us could fill the front and back of an entire sheet of paper in a 50-minute class period and still get As and Bs—except I couldn't write notes in Algebra. Our notes were dramatic, passionate, ridiculous. We described the moon, the stars, our tears, smiles and wishes. I used big words I didn't understand; she addressed me as "Dearest" and laced her letters with *thou*, *doth* and *shall*. She signed her notes *Solange* and I signed mine *Sergé*, our names from French class. Love, Solange or Love, Sergé—even when we were just friends, we already signed Love.

Claire was small and very curvy with bowed-out hips. Her hair was cut short and curled naturally, which she hated. "I have Mom hair," she said sometimes, pulling at the flat results in her rearview mirror. "You don't," I'd say, fiddling with things in her glove box, looking for a mixed tape I made her. But it was true, her haircut was the same as both of our mothers. She looked older than she was, like she was a mom of somebody, though she was only one year ahead of me in school. I looked younger than I was, like the effeminate pre-pubescent kid of somebody, although I was a sophomore.

Then one night there was a dance at her church; it had a celestial theme. Tall caged windows were covered with stiff blue paper and rubbed all over with glue and glitter. Moons and stars, comets and constellations dotted out in shiny silver marker. A slow song started when I was dancing with Angie, but I was switched and then dancing with Claire. This had all been planned though I wasn't aware of it at the time. The song was "I Can't Fight This Feeling" by REO Speedwagon and I hated it. Except I had to love it because it was now our song—Claire's and mine. We were close, Claire's cheek pressed to my shivering chest. She wore a thick sweater and under my hands I could tell she was sweating. The room was dark, crowded, loud, glittering and blue. We danced, sort of waddling in a vague circle. Left, pause, right, pause, left, pause, right, slowly rotating over some invisible point on the floor like an orbit. She knew she loved me right then but she wouldn't tell me until later.

After that, our notes changed. She would write every day and tell me how rapturously in love she was with me and I wrote the same back to her. I described my strong feelings and made many fantastical promises about moonlit walks, sunrises, New York weekends and European summers. Strangely, it was easy to write about these things but hard to talk about them. In those years, love wasn't any deeper than friendship. I knew what came along with love (sex) so I tried to avoid the topic altogether. To me, writing those feelings for her on paper was the way I could pretend that I was a boy with a girlfriend just like all the other boys—overlooking that other boys didn't write at least six page-long love notes every day at school.

Angie and I pack up our food and tape player, it's time to drive around. We love driving around. Her car is a Volkswagen Quantum; her dad bought it at a police auction for $200 after it was confiscated in a drug investigation. You can start it without the key by turning the ignition switch and the stereo works when the car isn't running. Driving around means more singing and it means seeing who's home. We zoom past our friends' houses, and if their cars aren't there, we make guesses, practice

conjecture. "Did he have to work today?" It's Saturday, we
have nothing better to do. Angie drives too fast, not slowing at
corners, whipping us to the sides of the car on purpose.

We have to sing this song, she says, and reaches under
my legs for her shoebox of tapes. It's Pink Floyd, "Wish You
Were Here." She knows all the words. I'm still learning, but
I know the chorus. Her car doesn't have air-conditioning, the
upholstery sticks to the backs of my legs. My bare feet are up
on the dashboard so I sit slouched in the seat, one hand out of
the car, buoyed by the breeze. She turns up the radio. "We're
just two lost souls swimming in a fish bowl, year after year." She
stabs her finger at me in the hot air, one point for every note.
This song means us.

We start talking about Claire again, how she's trying to get
with Kevin.

"She's always had a thing for him," Angie says, and then she
turns down her stereo. "No offense."

"Whatever." My hand is still riding the air. We want to do
something to Kevin, want him to know we know what's going
on. Because it's the middle of the afternoon, TP-ing his house
or finding a bunch of For Sale signs and sticking them in his
front yard are out. Angie suggests his car, we could cover it in
shaving cream or dish soap? "The Cherry Bars!" I shout. We
love it. Smear them on his car, a mess across the windshield. He
won't know it's us but he'll *know* it's us.

Claire once tied a silk scarf over my eyes and led me carefully down her basement steps. We'd been dating almost a year by then. She whispered *Ssh!* because her parents were already in bed. When her parents were home, her house was like a library—you had to be quiet because that was the rule. My socks slid the slightest bit on each painted step. At the bottom, we stood on the cement floor of her unfinished basement. "Here, this way," she said, and I was pulled over there. A crinkling of plastic and she let go of my hand. "Hold on," she said. I stood frozen and blind, heard the flick of a lighter, then the tiny hiss of flame. It was so quiet. She grabbed my hand again, pulled me forward, then down, my knees crushing a pile of pillows. "Okay," she said.

I slipped the scarf off my head and I wanted to check my hair because it felt messed up. But we were sitting on the floor wrapped in a shimmering bubble. Plastic painter's drop cloths hung from the ceiling, enclosing us, and strings of glowing white Christmas lights were wound up inside. Paper streamers and more drop cloths—shredded into long strips—hung down, moving and waving as we breathed. It was beautiful. She sat on a pillow too, a low table between us held dozens of candles, the little flames wiggled under our breath. There was no air. She reached behind her pillows and brought out a bottle of sparkling grape juice, the bottle that looked just like wine, and poured it into plastic cups.

"What is this?" I asked.

"Oh, nothing," she said, pretending to hide a coy smile that she wanted me to see. "I wanted to surprise you."

I hadn't noticed before but music was playing from somewhere in the corner, a low soft song. "I'm surprised, I guess," I shrugged because I couldn't think of what else to say. I didn't know what I was supposed to do.

At this time, Claire and I were comfortable hand-holders, but going any further made me nervous. Just staying Claire's best friend would have been my plan, if I were the one doing the planning, but she and Angie took care of that. In fact, nothing really changed for me between being Claire's friend and her boyfriend, except we held hands during movies, attended prom, spent Friday nights together, just us, and at the end of phone conversations and dates, we paused and said with purpose, "I love you." Beyond those three words, I never willingly talked about my feelings of our relationship—I only wrote about them. And if Claire noticed I could only write that I loved her, she didn't talk about it either.

By the night of the bubble in the basement, Claire thought it was a pretty big deal that we'd dated more than a year and never kissed or reached a hand up under a shirt or squeezed anything of each other's yet. My latest explanation for not kissing her—when it was demanded of me—was I imagined the moment of our first kiss so perfectly and it had to be just like my vision that the pressure was too much to live up to. Which worked. The truth was when I tried to picture Our First Kiss, I couldn't see anything. Not our faces or hands and certainly not what I was feeling.

After thirty minutes in the fragile quivering bubble, she had to drive me home to meet my curfew. "We better go," I said, and I hugged her, thanked her for my surprise.

Angie called the next morning. "You're so stupid," she said. "She was trying to set the mood for you. You were supposed to kiss her!"

Kevin is watching our friend Jon's dogs while his whole family is on vacation. If Kevin's car isn't at his own house, then he must be over there. We know he's not at work because his car isn't where he usually parks it at the mall. We already checked. The houses in Kevin's subdivision are small and shoved closely together. His dad is gone, divorced from his mom years ago and his sister is away at college. Kevin lives with just his mom and their two dogs that they both talk to in high voices.

It's been two months since Claire and I broke up and we haven't seen much of each other. Kevin and Angie just broke up just two weeks ago, and they still talk on the phone because they are trying to be friends. They want to get back together, I think but don't say to Angie. "I'm so glad to be done with him," she says, at the corner when we turn onto his street.

His car isn't there. We decide to drive by our vacationing friend's house. "We're going to give Kevin his 'just desserts.'" I chuckle at how clever I am. Angie nods but I don't think she's listening. I actually can't believe she is going along with this cherry bars thing because she still loves Kevin or thinks she does, though she'd never admit it. I don't hate Kevin or anything, though I am quietly jealous of him, and how he gets Angie all to himself when they're dating. The image of these bars spread on his car—gooey, red and mean—is secretly thrilling because it will be real proof to Kevin of my connection with Angie.

"We have to get there right now! Before he leaves," she says, pressing down on the gas pedal. Now that we have this idea, neither one of us can imagine not going through with it. We're actually already looking forward to this memory, how we'll laugh later about what we're about to do, and we haven't even gotten around to doing it. Quick curves, darting sprints, rushed stops at surprise red lights. There's a long slow trail of cars heading west to the hill on busy Elm Street where there is a steep drop on the other side. "We have to go," she says, and the engine works furiously under us as she pulls over the solid yellow line to pass them all.

We're on the wrong side of the street, speeding up the hill that we can't see over—a car coming at us or not, a kid chasing a lost softball or not, an anything or not. I suck in a breath like I'm leaping into a pool and I don't know how cold the water will be. My fingers squeeze tighter around the handle hanging from the Quantum's ceiling. Angie's arms are locked straight on the wheel, she's pressed back into the seat. No singing or laughing and I don't know what song is playing. We dive over the top of the hill and the road underneath us is empty. We speed down the slope, pass the slow cars; drivers' heads turn to see who could be so stupid. Nothing happens though because we're invincible. Our bodies and also our friendship. We have to live on past this ordinary afternoon or else we'd never know what a time it was, it was. I wave to the glancing drivers, Angie pulls the car back into the right lane. We both scream.

"We almost died this afternoon." I say it monotone like I'm bored though my neck is sweating. A minute goes by and so does a mile.

"The safternoon," she says.

We have a lot to talk about. That's what Claire's note said. She tucked it under my windshield wiper, in the parking lot of the YMCA where I worked as a Latchkey supervisor, my summer job. The facility was off the highway, off the service road, past several pastures of dry, leaning corn and empty barns—a long way from Claire's house. So this was serious. It was raining but the note was folded up and zipped inside a plastic sandwich bag. She'd drawn goofy faces on the note, big round eyes, tiny two-dot noses and open-mouthed grins. She didn't draw the shape of the heads around them, just the parts of faces, so they didn't look whole. One of them was crying, probably knowing it was over.

When I drove up, she was sitting on her porch. This was six

months after the night I was supposed to kiss her when I didn't kiss her. Her parents' cars weren't in the driveway but I still parked in the street because her mom thought my car leaked oil. Claire was sitting on a bench, her giant knitted sweater pulled over her feet, reading a paperback romance novel.

Inside the house, we were alone but the silence felt like a presence, like someone was in the room with us, hiding. She sat down in the living room, I sat beside her on the sofa and she started talking.

It was the usual thing: Our relationship didn't seem to be going anywhere. Yes, we got along really well, she related to me better than anyone else in her whole life, but it had been that way for so long and it didn't seem to be changing. She felt alone. She felt lonely. She felt like I didn't really love her because I didn't ever want to touch her, or kiss her, or have sex with her or whatever. She was sorry, she didn't mean that. But, yes, she did mean that. Was it her? Was she ugly? Or crazy? Why was she the only one who ever wanted to talk about this? She knew I thought about it too, but didn't think I *really* thought about it, not the way she did.

A long breath pushed out of her like something had been lifted or something had been taken away, I couldn't decide. She waited for me to talk.

I said maybe we shouldn't be in this relationship anymore.

"Are you sure?" she said.

"I am," I said. "I think I am."

She began to cry and I reached out my hand to touch her sweater, but she hopped off the sofa and ran upstairs. I heard scraping and bumping noises, the hollow sound of a closet door, then the heavy bumps of her heels hammered back down to me.

She handed me a big cardboard box. I recognized the markered goofy faces drawn all over the sides, the same goggly eyes and curled smiles. Dark capital letters warned PRIVATE PERSONAL MESSY OUTPOURINGS OF A NAKED SOUL! KEEP OUT!! I knew inside was every note I'd written her, probably every single one. Hundreds of them, sliding over each other as the box tilted in my hands. I never knew she was saving them all. It wasn't as heavy as I would have guessed.

"You have to take this," she said.

"Why?"

"You have to." She sniffled.

"I can't."

"You have to. I can't have these anymore."

"I wrote them to you. These are for you." We sat on the couch again, side by side. I set the box between my feet, opened the lid and saw all the notes. I noticed for the first time everything in Claire's house was white. The carpet, the sectional sofa, the vertical blinds, the rugs, the coffee table, the frames on the walls and then the note in my hand, the whole box of notes on the floor. She couldn't look at me. I couldn't stop looking at the carpet.

After a few silent minutes, I leaned over and awkwardly

hugged her because I wanted to leave. The sooner I was out of that quiet white house, the better. I stood and she picked up the box again and I told her I wasn't taking the notes. She slumped down as I yanked the front door open. On the long sofa, she somehow looked smaller than she was. Her sweater was pulled down over her knees and she gripped a crumpled tissue. I wanted to go but I also didn't want to leave her alone. If we drove around and listened to *Solitude* maybe she'd feel better. I told her I'd call her but she didn't say anything bac

On the passenger seat in my car was her note in the plastic bag, the one asking me to come here, the last one she'd ever write to me. Her words were so important, she couldn't take her chances with the storm rolling around above us. Like she protected every note I wrote in her big box with the goofy faces standing guard. Every note was a different hour of the day when I loved her, or wrote to her that I did.

Part of the reason I couldn't take that box from her was taking the notes would mean I'd finally have to take responsibility for them. I knew all along I wasn't being honest with Claire when I wrote to her I loved her or suggested names for the quadruplets she was convinced we'd have. Taking back the notes would be like taking back the feelings depicted on them, and they were always already hers. And it wasn't that I didn't feel anything for Claire—I loved her very much—as my friend. Because I had such a hard time talking about my feelings, the notes were her only evidence of our relationship.

She collected them all hoping the accumulation would equal the physical affection she desired from her thin, high-voiced boyfriend who borrowed her *Phantom of the Opera* soundtrack and memorized all the words.

With her last note in my hand, I stared back at her front door and thought about her sitting there. I wished she didn't have to be in that sad white house where everything looked perfect but nothing was. Her dad was very sick, there was something wrong in his kidneys and he needed dialysis treatments every day. I remembered how one morning before school started, she and I sat together in a quiet hallway and she said, "I don't know what I would do if I didn't have you." I asked her what she meant. She opened her mouth almost immediately to answer but didn't say anything. We sat mute until the bell rang a minute later, and I always wondered what her answer might have been.

"Cold cuts will take the paint off a car, if the sun is hot enough." I've heard this somewhere, and just knowing it makes me sound as if I am capable of such a thing. The car windows are rolled down, Angie's hair is flying all around her face like she's underwater. Houses, cars and lawns blur past us. We drive to Jon's house where we hope Kevin will be, around a narrow curve, up a slow hill. We're chanting "BE THERE! BE THERE!" with tight red faces. I'm bouncing the container of cherry bars on my lap, wet residue streaking the inside of the lid in sugary ridges. One more turn right, one left, and there's the house, at the mouth of a dead-end court. Kevin's car *is* there, as if we summoned it, as if we screamed, willed and commanded it there. This is perfect. We can almost see his face when he trots out to his car after piling up the family's mail in the kitchen and calling the dogs back inside, and there, across his windshield is the weirdest mess he's ever seen. My grandma's homemade cherry bars as vandalism. The stereo plays the fast chorus of The Carpenters' "We've Only Just Begun," because it's true.

As we turn in the cul-de-sac, though, we see them. Kevin and Claire, both of them, walking out of the house, staring at Angie and me. We look at each other because we thought we were summoning his car, and accidentally we summoned him, and Claire too. On their faces are smiles until they stop smiling because we look so ridiculous, chanting and screaming out of the open windows. They don't know what we're up to, but it's pretty obvious that whatever it is, they're on the wrong side of it.

Seeing them side by side, I realize something I can't ever tell Angie. I don't want to rub these cherry bars on Kevin's car as a message about him and Claire because it's not him that I care about. My actual concern is that Claire cannot date anyone ever because I don't want her next boyfriend—if it's Kevin or anybody else—to start kissing her. That would be the explanation to everyone that what was wrong with Claire and I was me. That's why Kevin and Claire can't get together. That's why it's actually fine that Angie still likes Kevin, and for her, these cherry bars are some kind of bizarre flirtation. That's why

I must believe that Angie and I have only just begun to live because only I know my hidden difficult secrets. I'm already nostalgic for our present because the future is so impossible.

In front of Jon's house, Angie pulls her car over, jams it into park and switches off the engine. "Get down," she whispers. "Hide. Pretend you're sleeping." This sounds reasonable at this moment, even though Claire and Kevin have just seen us drive past them, just seen our dumb, surprised faces. We slump down into the foot wells and curl up. I shove the cherry bars under the seat—they are a dead giveaway. Angie fits under her steering wheel. My face is crammed between my knees, I can't see anything. As Kevin and Claire walk closer to the car, I reach up and turn off the music.

Tightrope

. . . . .

One of the smart mouths is showing off but we're ignoring him. He's attempting a tricky shot when he trips and wrecks on the gymnasium floor. His smug face squeaks across the polished wood and the noise ricochets off the cinderblock walls along with the other kids' voices. I do my best not to notice because I'm close to winning my Solitaire game. Lisa, the other supervisor in the gym right now sits across the table from me snapping down her own cards. Neither of us likes the fallen smart mouth or any of the others in his crew, and we smirk at his comeuppance. I'm 17 years old and after this summer, I'll be a senior in high school. Lisa's older, a college student somewhere. All the supervisors here at the Y think she's too weird to talk to, except me.

We've got seventy-eight children between five and fourteen years old under our charge. To get this job, I was supposed to be eighteen, but my mom knew the director so he bent the rules. If anybody asks, I've been instructed to lie, but I have a hard time keeping my story straight. I'm a short pale guy with skinny wrists, pink knees, and a boy's high, unchanged voice. A couple of the smart mouths look older than I do.

Despite my obvious young age and small body, Lisa is considered the misfit of all the supervisors. Her hair is dyed an unusual reddish-brown like apple juice and she draws on her eye makeup asymmetrically—one eye outlined in black with a dramatic, pointed corner, the other lid shadowed darkly like a bruise. But as exotic as her makeup might be, her clothes are plain and somewhat sloppy: dark long-sleeve T-shirts, soft jeans, scuffed sneakers with beautiful designs drawn in glitter. It's this contradiction that I find so mysterious and irresistible.

In fact, the other supervisors leave Lisa and me to ourselves and I savor the idea that they associate me with her. We're not really friends, but lately we have begun to talk more about books and music. She let me borrow a CD of hers where a woman moaned out a song about being raped and it sounded so theatrical and sophisticated, it thrilled me even if I didn't entirely understand it. Lying on the floor in my bedroom, I listened to the song repeating for hours until my Dad shoved his face through the door. "*What* are you listening to?"

Lisa gives up on Solitaire, and as she reshuffles, she asks where I'm going back to college. I confess finally I'm only a high school senior.

"Oh, really," she says, not looking so surprised. "Where do you go?"

I tell her. It's one of a few high schools in our suburban Missouri town near St. Louis.

"One of my best friends used to go there. He finished last year."

I ask who. "Justin Curtis," she says. "Do you know him?"

"Yes!" As shy as I am, it feels like a miracle that we actually know the same person, even if my school isn't very big. Most of my friends are other theater kids—a whole group of us who devote our after-school hours to acting like other people. The revelation that I know her friend Justin feels like one more link in our emerging connection. I didn't know him well but I'm not about to tell Lisa.

Justin and I were on the school newspaper staff together when I was a freshman but I haven't talked to him since that year. He was as much a misfit in our school as Lisa is here at the Y. He was a tall and skinny boy—skinnier and paler than me. Where I look underdeveloped and puny, Justin's thinness and whiteness appeared anemic, sickly. His shoulders pulled together in front of his chest. He brushed his hair in a pouf in front, where it was dyed blonde, and then in back where the natural brown color showed through, it was cut shorter and swooped down in a curly tail that he nervously fingered. His lips were pink and chapped because he never closed his mouth, almost as if he was unable to breathe through his nose; he seemed to stare and quietly pant like he was always waiting for something to end so he could go.

But more than just his hair made Justin a misfit. His soft, girlish voice, sounding like a string of whimpers rather than sentences or words, and his limp walk. He was often called a certain word—in the newspaper room, the hallways at school, and probably in his classes. I recognized the word because it was also sometimes called out to me. I always felt it land on my skin with a sting but I found if I pretended I didn't hear it then I could also pretend I didn't know what it meant.

The smart mouths in the gym with Lisa and me will grow into the kind of kids who use that awful word. The one who fell down earlier is in front of us now, showing us the long pink mark on his arm. Lisa and I have no sympathy. We know who this kid is so we don't care. He walks off discouraged, throwing his arm around, muttering under his breath.

"So," Lisa says, once he's gone. "Would you want Justin to call you or something? I'm sure he'd want to hear from you."

"Sure!" I say. "It would be nice to hear from him too."

By the time Justin calls several weeks later, my final year of high school is underway and lonely. My best friend Angie is back with her boyfriend Kevin for the third time. They are utterly devoted to this renewed relationship so they spend every Friday and Saturday night together, just the two of them. For the first month of the new year, on weekend nights, I shamble around the house throwing myself on the sofa, staring at the phone, my pathetic hopeful voice already recorded on Angie's parents' answering machine pleading for her to call. If I'm feeling up to it, I lie across my bedroom carpet and doodle or write poems about despair and hardship. One particularly inspiring Friday night, on a notebook illustrated with teardrops, I discover that the words "bedroom" and "boredom" share all the same letters. My mother watches with concern, suggests mall trips or movies but it's no use—to be seen with her in public is worse than being alone. My only choice is to wait for Angie's inevitable tearful phone call delivering the news that she and Kevin are finished, that's it, and I should come over immediately.

If I was normal I'd go on my own dates but I'm not so I don't. I'm not interested in dating, though I did have a girlfriend for almost a year but that didn't go anywhere mostly because I didn't let it. At school, I see how students pair off, this girl for that boy, but there's no similar impulse inside me. I want to be around girls—particularly Angie, if Kevin would leave her alone—I just don't want anything more. There's something different between me and them—the boys paired with girls. And as much as I am intimidated by those tall and loud young men who barrel down the school hallways, I'm still drawn to them, interested not by being left out, but because I want to watch and memorize the way their bodies strut and shout. I know there's something deeper and more complicated to my inchoate urges but I do my best to ignore it. Years from now, I'll see that by not dating at all—after that first girlfriend, whom I never even kissed—I could successfully sidestep the whole question of who I wanted to date without having to think very hard about why.

I answer the phone one night after school and it's Justin. When he asks for me, I recognize his strange voice even after two years and the inside of my throat suddenly feels fat. I know how he would sound to my parents. His voice sounds so small, almost child-like. But it doesn't bother me the way it would bother my family and I bask in my surprisingly mature outlook, very special for a boy my age. I'm afraid they'll overreact again like the time my mother wouldn't let me join my theater friends for ice skating in St. Louis because she thought the area was too dangerous. "There are a lot of gangs over there," she said. "At the ice rink?" I asked, mocking her. "Ice skating gangs! Oh, Mother," I said, shaking my head and performing a loud patronizing laugh that was supposed to change her mind, but didn't.

As Justin and I talk, it's clear that he is nervous, but I don't understand why. My words steer our conversations, which we share for four days in a row. After we trade a few sentences about Lisa, her music and glitter-doodled shoes, all I can think to talk about are those days in the newspaper room. Does he remember this person, that day or this time? He answers my questions, then waits for more. When seconds of quiet stretch between us, I blurt out dumb stories about school, or the current newspaper room where I'm an editor. He begins asking questions and I answer them, and he asks more. He's not hiding, he's just not revealing as much as I am, and I'm too young to understand why. And though his calls are never planned, when the ring is heard throughout our house, I'm always first to answer. My thirteen-year-old brother Garrett generally monitors most of my calls with the phone in his room. This is the phase when he thinks he's my father. Each time Justin and I talk this week, I listen for the fumbling or breathing that always gives Garrett away, but I don't hear it.

Finally, on the fourth evening, Justin asks if I'd like to do something with him, the next day if possible, which is Friday. I'm free, I say, because, of course Angie's heart and weekend belong to Kevin. "What do you feel like doing?" I ask.

"You know what I haven't done in years?" he says, his voice somehow now sounding more like a young boy's than ever. "And it happens to be in town, I heard a commercial on the radio. . . ."

I'm not sure if I'm supposed to guess so I stay quiet.

"Let's go to the circus," he says.

About an hour before he's supposed to pick me up the following evening, I've told my mother only that I'm doing something with a guy from newspaper who graduated the previous year. She asks millions of questions. She's so unused to the idea that I would want to spend time with anyone but Angie, she's immediately curious. But even more surprising, it's with another boy—an activity she's been suggesting for years. To my mother's mind, I spend too much time with girls, and "hanging out with the guys" is just what I need to nudge my dormant interests in dating, sports and yard work to sudden bright life. But I know Justin isn't the guy she has in mind so I tell her about the Lisa connection, restating though that this is a guy I knew in newspaper and we were friends then and he's coming to pick me up soon, and I'm not really sure what we're doing tonight, but yes, I'll be home by midnight, the curfew. I wait in the driveway, set for a quick getaway.

Of course I haven't seen Justin for two years so I have no idea what he'll look like, though I know how he sounds, and that's not good. When his car turns in, I see his same strained face and open mouth, the hardened eyes and the white arms gripping the steering wheel. I yell into the house, "He's here! Bye!" and scurry across the pavement, running up to Justin's car before he's pressed down his brake. I stand at the passenger side door and peer in. He smiles. His hair is cut short and practically "normal" in terms of my mother's standards except he's dyed it a shiny auburn the color of an Irish setter. He shifts into park and unlocks my door. My mother steps out of the house into the garage.

"Wait a minute," she says, her flattened hand rising to her brow to make an awning for her face. "I want to meet your friend."

I stand helplessly next to the car as Justin looks at her, looks at me and then looks at her again when she marches across the driveway. He unlatches his seatbelt, pushes open the door, and stands in front of my mother. He's taller and knobbier than I remembered, wearing a skintight Polo shirt and creased brown pants. He offers his hand to her and she moves her eyes from his Irish setter head to his shabby loafers and back again.

"Mom, Justin. Justin, Mom," I say, staring at my shoes, watching one of them take a small step toward the car.

The brown Missouri river separates St. Charles from St. Louis. There's a long bridge to cross, a hulking contraption of grey girders and dark rivets that looks like a giant skeleton. As far back as I can remember, when riding across the bridge, I've held my breath. It's a bargain I've struck with God—our family car can make it to the other side without the bridge collapsing into the ugly water if I can hold my breath the whole time. Maybe if I paid more attention on Sunday mornings in church, I'd know this isn't the way God really works, or that's what my mother would say if she noticed me turning red in the back of the mini-van. To hold my breath now at this age feels silly but after so many years and so many safe trips, it's become my superstition.

Across the river, St. Louis is a marvelous city but it's full of dangers and I'm not allowed to go there without my parents. So I lie and go anyway when my friends are willing to drive. In St. Louis, there's a neighborhood I've visited only a few times that I'm drawn to, a place that feels risky but also cool. *I* don't feel cool necessarily, but I feel that coolness is nearby and available. In this neighborhood is Café Chaos. You sit on dirty furniture and sip tea while coughing in an incense cloud, music howling from ripped speakers. Above you, each ceiling tile is hand-painted in vivid swirling colors depicting Technicolor teddy bears, Chinese symbols, and Che Guevara. It's too loud to hear your companions so you just sit and stare. I particularly like what being there says about me. Even the name contradicts everything I know; the supposed serenity of "Café" colliding with volatile "Chaos." At the moment, it is my favorite place anywhere and I've only been once.

Like the bright white ice rink, my mother thinks this area of the city is deadly though I don't believe she's ever seen it. I've mentioned it cautiously with her, just to confirm that she thinks I shouldn't hang out there.

"You want to go where?" she said, turning off her Game Boy and setting it down to give my interest in this neighborhood her full attention.

"Oh, I don't want to *go* there. I'm just wondering if you've ever been. It's supposed to be pretty cool." I shrugged, like I was only making conversation, as though her answer didn't matter.

"I'm sorry my mom is such a dork. She gets hyper about everything," I say. Justin and I are driving on the highway toward St. Louis to eat somewhere before the circus. Justin hasn't said much since we started. So I'm making inane comments about radio songs or pointing out that everything in St. Charles is beige just to have something to say. My hands don't know where to go, in my lap or beside my thighs on the seat, or one propped up by the window and one on the armrest. I test the possibilities but nothing feels right. Justin knows a diner near the arena where we'll see the circus. "That sounds good," I say. " I love diners." Once I hear my sentence, I know how ridiculous it sounds. I'm trying to seem interesting by being a lover of diners—when I don't even know if it's true. Steak'N'Shake might be the only diner I've been to.

In fact, Justin's diner looks nothing like Steak N'Shake. His place has greasy front windows, wood paneling and a black and white linoleum floor. There are two spots at the counter so we sit side by side while an enormous black man takes our order. His head is pinched in a white paper cap, dark stains smeared across his apron. Justin warns me the food here isn't much; he comes here for atmosphere. We order and Justin lights a cigarette.

My stool is bolted to the floor so it's difficult to turn like I want to. Behind me in the corner, old men grumble with yellowed moustaches. Near the door, some teenagers slouch at a table blowing soda bubbles with their straws. There's a kid running around with untied shoes. Sizzling noises fry out the background and I'm stuck facing the dirty open kitchen as Justin's smoke mingles with the smell of bacon.

"This is a cool place," I say. I've got the hands problem again, where to put them, what they should do. Something has shoved me off balance, forcing me to be aware of my body. I start wondering why I'm so uncomfortable—if it's the diner, the way my mother unnerved me with her suspicious eyes, or just the unfamiliarity of sitting somewhere on this side of the river.

"It's nice," he says, knocking ash off his cigarette. "I come here a lot."

Which isn't hard to imagine. With the way he looks and talks, Justin has to be used to not fitting in. But who really fits in here? This diner is the place for all the people that don't fit in at all the other places. He smashes his cigarette into the ashtray and reaches for his pack, but puts it down. He folds his arms over his chest, unfolds them and smoothes out his pants. He's having the hands problem too.

"Have you talked to Lisa this week?" I ask.

"Who?" he says, swiveling to face me. "Oh, I keep forgetting she's Lisa to you."

"What do you mean?"

"Just that she's Charlie too. To some people she's Lisa and to some people she's Charlie. Usually she's Charlie to me."

I want to ask him what the difference is and how he knows which one he's talking to. I'm also trying to understand how she's able to hold two names and intriguing personalities inside herself simultaneously when I can barely manage to be interesting as one person. This must have something to do with the juxtaposition of her strange face and ordinary clothes—Lisa must wear the jeans and shirts, Charlie has the Cleopatra eyes.

I envy her ability to decide. Actually my association with people like she and Justin is my own attempt at being somebody else. There seem to be ways that the people in glamorous leather jackets and ripped jeans conceal themselves and stand out from the crowd at the same time. My appearance is so ordinary in my over-sized T-shirts—my mom buys all my clothes—jeans, and Converse sneakers and I still look like the kind of boy I don't want to be.

When we arrive at the circus, I'm instantly aware we shouldn't be here. All around are families, families, families. At this arena, I've previously seen soccer games, Sesame Street Live and a monster truck rally but each time legitimately, with my mom, dad and brother. I can't tell if Justin knows how clearly we don't fit in. At the diner, the place where no one seemed to belong, it was fine to sit next to him. But at the circus, the sight of the two of us is as lurid and outlandish as the sequined lady will be dangling from her trapeze. Two of us at the circus is one too many. Despite the giant size of the arena, as we settle into our seats surrounded on all sides by parents and kids spilling popcorn and waving fiber optic wands, the place is somehow claustrophobic; I feel the grip of how much I don't want to be here.

The lights drop, the room swells in applause and screams, a spotlight cuts through the dark and explodes on the floor. The ringmaster steps into the beam, his voice booms over us, the circus begins. Sparkle, smoke, elephants, tigers, stilt-walkers and stuntmen—it's actually reassuring that the show is so predictable.

Justin claps easily at the acrobatic leaps, the man shot out of the cannon, the car crammed with clowns. If he's uncomfortable, he doesn't show it. The families pressing in against us don't bother him. But I can barely watch what he's doing or focus on the circus because I'm listening for that word—the word we've both been called, always singularly, but now I'll hear it in plural with an incriminating and dangerous *s*. My neck is tense, I hold my spine absolutely still, thinking if I don't move, no one will notice the spectacle of us. And as impossible as it would be to hear, I search the crowd noise for the word anyway: the quick rasp of the first syllable, then the snag of the middle, how my ear gets caught on the doubled *g*, and finally, the sudden twisting down of the last part like a barb on a hook, how all by itself the ending sounds like the place in my body where the whole word hits me when it's called out like my name.

After the circus, we make our way through the family crowd to Justin's car and sit in the parking lot to decide what to do next. I wish he'd just take me home, but I play along with his suggestions. Besides, going home now is too early—my mom is certainly still playing Game Boy, listening to the news. I'd rather tiptoe in after she's gone to bed. He suggests going to his place and there's little to do but agree.

Justin lives in what's called a boxcar apartment: a cramped rectangle where you walk through the living room to get to the bedroom and then through the bedroom to get to the kitchen. He pushes open his front door fortified with iron bars. In the living room are a sofa, several wooden chairs, a coffee table and Madeline Luff. When I see her smoking and talking to another girl in Justin's boxcar, my puzzled eyes round out and I gawk at her like she's a movie star. In fact, five years earlier when I was in junior high, Madeline Luff was the closest thing I knew to a movie star. She was the girl who dressed completely in black, every day only in rich, complicated black skirts, dresses and coats. Her hair wasn't naturally black but she dyed it, the same opaque black of ink—so dark that light couldn't reflect off it, like her head was a black hole. Then, she painted and powdered her face white. Our school newspaper featured her in our ongoing series about unique students. Whenever I passed her inky figure in the hallway clamor, I wanted to stop and stare. Now what's stranger to me than her wearing only black every day of junior high school is that she doesn't look that way anymore; she's changed—her face is bare and her clothes are in color.

"Hi, J," she says. She's the roommate. Her voice sounds ordinary and therefore disappointing. I stand next to Justin and pretend that seeing her is normal. She stubs out her cigarette and her friend nods, a serious blond wearing dark red lipstick.

"This is Ryan," he says, and I lift my hand and wave, a gesture that immediately feels silly. Both sets of their eyes scan me from shoes to hair. Madeline doesn't seem to recognize me though I look almost like I did in junior high, except I'm a few inches taller. Smoke shoots from her nostrils while she and her friend glance at each other. On a squat table between their knees sit two glasses of red wine.

"Well, what are you boys up to this evening?" the blond asks. She's clutching her arms because it's cold in here and her dress is missing its sleeves.

"We went to the circus," Justin answers then heads to the kitchen. I stand there in the center of the room like I just dropped through the ceiling from another apartment. Justin freezes in the doorway and turns around. "Oh, do you want something to drink? We have wine."

"Water, please!" I nearly sing it, projecting to the four bare walls closing in on me. Besides three fiery sips of champagne at a rural cousin's wedding reception held in a school gym, I've never drunk alcohol. None of my friends have either. I've never even been to a party. In fact, my experience is so limited, when I think of people my age drinking, I envision watery, dramatic images from public service announcements of mangled cars and teen funerals. The idea that someone almost handed me a glass of wine unsteadies my legs. I'm suddenly aware I'm somewhere I probably shouldn't be and something terrible is certain to happen.

"Here you are," Justin says, handing me my glass of water, which I drink down in gulps. He pops open a Diet Coke. I stop holding my breath and sit in a chair that squeals when I fall into it. I don't know where to look—at Madeline, the serious friend, Justin or at the features of the apartment. When I set down my glass, my eyes notice a book in the rubble of scattered papers on the table; on the cover is a man's bare torso.

I guess this book belongs to Justin because I guess he must be gay. I've recently discovered photographs of men like this inside my Dad's running catalogs—inflated muscles, tiny shorts and wet forearms. Sometimes when I'm home alone, I take the catalogs to my bedroom, but when I look at the men behind my closed door, it must be different than the way Justin looks at them. I've fooled myself into believing that when I stare deeply at those bodies, I feel something other than desire and I'm naive enough to believe the pictures appeal to me because I'm interested in how my own body might look one day, if I ever start looking like a man.

I ask Justin about the bathroom and he points through the bedroom to the kitchen. "It's all the way to the end," he says, his thin hand waving me down. Walking through their bedroom, with its pair of unmade beds, an ironing board jutting out and clothes scattered all around, I think living here would be the opposite of my house. At home, we each have our own rooms and hide in our own favorite corners. Here in Justin's apartment, everything is out for everyone. This must be how people live in the city—not enough walls and no place for secrets.

Walking back to the front room, I notice an open shoebox

full of syringes on the ironing board. There are bright orange tips snapped over the needles. Next to them, huddled in a corner of the box are glass bottles full of clear liquid with typed words on their sides. This box can mean only one thing. I don't want Justin or Madeline to see me gaping so I keep my pace and walk back to the living room, but my mind suddenly crowds with panicked thoughts, all of them melodramatic and illogical: someone in the room is a drug addict; I'm in the house of a drug addict; *I just went to the circus* with a drug addict.

When I imagined the possibilities of the city, of befriending people at chaotic cafes and diners, I overlooked these unexpected dangers my mother predicted. This may as well be the drive-by shooting at the ice skating rink. The fact that she was right burns inside me; it heats up my legs so I keep shifting my butt in the squeaky chair, barely able to sit. I nod or smile as the conversation moves on, putting forward the smallest effort while hinting that I don't want to be there. I turn down offers for refills of water. I yawn dramatically several times. Justin finally asks if I'm ready to go. "Oh," I say, hopping up. "Only if you are."

The car ride out of the city seems longer than the one in and that's usually the opposite. There are whole sections of the highway I don't recognize, strange billboards popping up one after the other making the deserted road stretch out. A few cars speed by, but mainly it's Justin and me puttering through alternating patches of light and dark along the highway. I've stopped trying to fill the quiet with conversation and now our silence sits between us like a third passenger.

And though the plain truth of the evening is beginning to emerge, it won't fully form while I'm waiting for the bridge that will mean we've finally crossed over to the safer side of things. What does become clear is I put myself here by pretending to be somebody I'm not. By letting Lisa believe Justin and I were better friends than we were. By saying I enjoy music that confuses me. By pretending I yearn for the experience of cities when actually I'd rather sit in my boredom where everything is familiar, unbarred, and well lit. Clusters of trees huddle like black clouds near the highway and the dead fish smell of the river slides into the car. I know that after a mile, we'll cross the water back into St. Charles.

Justin begins talking as we enter the mouth of the bridge. "I had a nice time tonight. I hope you did too." His voice is almost too soft to hear over the rhythmic bumping of the tires along the segments of the bridge. The water is black, heavy barges with winking lights drift slowly below. I say that I had a nice time too. The green sign posted at the end of the bridge begins to glow at the margin of Justin's headlights. The words aren't yet visible but I know them anyway: Now Entering St. Charles.

"I think finding nice guys to date around here is really hard, you know?"

I don't know how it happened but I forgot to hold my breath the one time it feels possible that the bridge will collapse.

My heart starts beating so hard I can hear my hot blood thumping through my ears. Suddenly all the air and saliva that make my mouth work disappear and so do all the words that I need to say to Justin because he's got this whole thing so wrong. And he must have gotten it wrong from Lisa. The effeminate kid who doesn't do normal boy things was the identity I was trying to obscure with this cooler one. I tried to create a new version of myself by hanging out with people like Lisa and Justin but now I know I just look like the kid I was trying to erase.

"I'm not gay," I say.

Justin sits there, staring, and I try to look at him, pushing my eyeballs as far left as they will strain so it won't look like I'm looking at him, but I can only make out his white wrists and the light blur of his shirt.

"Oh," he says, once we drive on and pass two more exits. "I'm sorry."

In his pause, I uncover the reason for Justin's anxiety tonight, and probably also my mother's, though for a much different reason. Everyone knew I was on a date but me.

"It's okay," I tell him. "That kind of thing actually happens a lot."

My curfew is midnight, and as I walk into the kitchen, the clock on the stove lets me know I'm ten minutes early. The family room is still lit up so my mom must not be in bed though I don't hear any TV sounds. Our German shepherd naps on his rug. He raises his heavy head, recognizes me, and flops back to sleep. I step over him into the family room. My mother and brother sit side by side on the sofa and in Garrett's Indian-style lap is my high school yearbook from last year.

"We need to talk to you," my mother says. She points to the cushion on the love seat where I always sit anyway. The TV is on but muted. Garrett opens the yearbook to a particular page and holds it to his chest. She's wearing her glasses and her nightgown. He's wearing a stretched-out T-shirt of my Dad's and a pair of boxer shorts, his orange hair is damp but parted straight and combed. My father would have gone to bed hours ago.

"Your brother found this," she says, taking the yearbook and turning it around to me.

I know what's on the page even before it's turned. There's a grid of headshots of the senior class and she points to Justin. It's a picture I saw last year when we got our yearbooks during the final week of school, and at that time, I laughed at his picture, so strange and so funny. But now, after the circus and the shoebox, looking at the photograph in front of her actually makes me queasy. In his square, Justin stares at the camera with a kind of contempt though it's hard to see because his hair is a black mess hanging over his face. I can see his lips, his open panting mouth, the way he is so obviously not smiling as if he doesn't have to. This is a mug shot of a criminal and now I'm guilty of something by association.

"I guess what we'd like to know is why you'd want to hang out with a person like this?"

The longer I stare at Justin's photo, the sillier he looks. With his black hair and empty face, he's a parody of danger instead of seeming capable of any true harm. But the fact that he wanted to look this way gets to me. I think of that awful word again and realize that Justin really *is* one—he's actually trying to be.

My brother leans over the book to look at the picture again; he turns from the photo and he and my mother grimace on cue. "We just think he's really creepy," she says.

There's nothing to do but nod and stay quiet. I reach to take my yearbook but Garrett won't hand it over. I turn and watch the TV for a few seconds even though I can't hear what the people are saying.

"Why is he still up?" I say, not facing them. "He shouldn't be involved in my business."

"What did you do tonight?" she asks.

I want to ask her what she imagined, what was the worst possibility she pictured during their long evening of scrambling through my bedroom, riffling through yearbooks. What dangers did she think I found myself in—me, the kid with the squeakiest clean of reputations, the boy who's never smoked a cigarette or been drunk or kissed anyone, who has never had a detention or even a tardy. I'm a little thrilled by the acts they imagine me capable of. They believe in the new identity I tried on tonight even if no one else does.

"I don't know," I say.

"Where did you go?" she presses me.

"You know, we drove around. It's not a big deal."

"Then why can't you tell us what you did with this person?"

"Well, first we drove out of the driveway, then we turned left. At the stop sign, we turned left again." I stand up, signaling I'm ready to go to my room. "Is that what you want?"

Garrett shakes his head as my mother's lips twist into a smirk. I've become the smart mouth, the one who says things that make other people wish they could see me fall. Garrett slams shut the yearbook and lets it slide off the sofa onto the floor. He's disappointed; he'd hoped for more of a punishment, something to make his investigation worth his effort. None of us knows what to say. The slick book falls and balances against the sofa on one of its corners, looking like it should topple but it doesn't.

"Well, you can't hang out with him again, I hope you know that," my mother says.

"I didn't know you were telling me who I could be friends with now," I say, leaning down to pick up my book. As I straighten myself up, eye level with Garrett, I say, "Stay out of my room."

My mother says, "Leave your brother alone."

I leave them standing there and walk down the long hallway to my end of the house. They watch me as I go and though I'm performing a confident hot-shit strut, I feel as if I'm inching along a tightrope and I've made the mistake of looking down.

In my dark room, I lie across the bed and start talking to God. *Please make Justin go away.* Through my closed door, I hear my mother and brother talking about what to do with me. I don't know if my prayer will work because I've been asking Him for years to take away the part of me that's like Justin, and it looks like He hasn't come through. And though Justin won't ever call my house again, I will see him once more, in a gas station parking lot, two years from this evening. By that time I'll know from another mutual friend that he's in fact not a heroin addict but a diabetic, and he shoots insulin into his own white arm every day.

But because it will be another four years before I'm able to admit the truth about myself, as I see him striding across the pavement, I turn off my car beside the gas pump and feel the same fear as at the circus. Carefully, I unlatch the lever that adjusts my seat and lie down slowly, all the way back. I stare at the ceiling of my car, wait for him to go somewhere—anywhere—and trust again that a held breath is enough to keep me safe.

The Men from Town

• • • • •

My brother Garrett owns three cell phones, and he's talking on two of them as he speeds down a rural highway in the middle of winter. I'm older than him by four years and sitting beside him with a plastic container of cookies balanced on my lap. I've been telling him to slow down his giant truck because he's not really paying attention to the road. He hangs up both phones and tosses them across his dashboard, and in the first moment of silence we've had in about thirty miles, I ask if he's sure he remembered to pack the new shoes we bought him the night before. He remembered the new coat, I'm certain, I can see it hanging back there, but the shoebox isn't visible. "Fuck yes, I already told you!" he shouts. It's the fourth time I've asked. Reaching across the cab, I tuck the peeking tag of his sweatshirt back under his collar.

We're driving to meet my parents at my grandparents' farm so we can bury my grandfather in two days. He died of a heart attack yesterday in his nursing home, though it seems as if he's been gone a few years now because he'd already lost his mind to Alzheimer's. He was my father's father, a farmer for many decades, a mandolin player in a bluegrass band, a leader in his basement church and tiny town—a lonely spot in the otherwise blank northeastern corner of Missouri's map—and the man with the largest hands I've ever seen.

My brother and I have our parents' dog with us. They rushed up to the farm as soon as they found out about my grandfather, to be with my grandmother and help plan the visitation and funeral. Now it's our job to bring their carsick golden retriever. My parents got this dog after I moved out, so I don't know her very well, and she's as nervous about riding in this truck as I am. At twenty-two, my brother still lives at home, so he knows her but doesn't really like her. Before we left, I forced some kind of Dramamine for dogs down her throat, but when Garrett takes some of these tight curves quickly, I can still hear her whine.

One of his phones starts ringing, so he grabs it off the dash and looks at the little lit-up screen. "It's Mom," he says, shoving the phone in my face so I can see her name. Just before he answers it, he clamps the antenna between his teeth and pulls it out. She's calling to ask how much longer it will be before we get there. "Hour," he says. "We got to get gas before long." My brother's voice is octaves deeper than mine. He listens another few seconds, then says, "No. One hour. Just hold your damn horses." When he hangs up the phone, he shakes his head at me, and sighs. "Fuck."

On down the highway, he pulls off at an exit where we have to drive a couple of empty miles before reaching the gas station. "Why did you pick this ghost town?" I ask, glancing across the road from our station to an ancient, derelict one, bristly weeds poking through the pavement in holes where gas pumps used to sit. He gives his reliable sneer at my reliable attitude problem and gets out to pump. This is February, so cold that in two days, on the morning we all huddle at the gravesite, a record will be set for low temperatures. My dad will tell me a story about a funeral he attended as a boy in the same cemetery on a similarly grey and freezing day when it was so cold that all the men parked their cars—these were the kind that had to be cranked by hand to start—but left their engines running through the ceremony.

Garrett opens the truck door and leans in, letting in a lot of wind, and throws two twenty-dollar bills in my lap. "Go pay," he says.

I pick up the twenties and lay them on his seat. "You do it," I say. "I don't want to go in." Over his shoulder, inside the squat gas-station store, the cashier sits on a stool and stares at us, smoking his cigarettes and wearing one of those hunter's caps with the bright orange that means watch out.

My brother pinches the twenties between his fingers, waves them from one corner, and drops them back in my lap. "Don't you have to go piss?"

"I can wait, thanks," I say, rolling down my window and holding my hand out, letting his bills flap in the wind as if I'm about to toss them free.

"All right, all right," he says, grabbing my arm and pulling it back into the cab.

Inside the station, he stands for a couple of minutes talking to the orange-hat man—about what, I can't imagine. Shifting from one foot to the other, his big frame swaying in front of the cashier's counter, he scratches his red beard, laughing. While he's in there, I undo my seatbelt and lean into the back to check for his shoes.

Once we arrive at my grandparents' farm, Garrett wrangles the dog while I carry in our suits, zipped together in the same garment bag, and my container of cookies. When I see my dad's only sister and my mother, they announce they have the perfect job for me. I'm handed a booklet provided by the funeral home, and as people come by and drop off food for us, it will be my task to log in who brings what, and to affix numbered stickers to any dishes we'll need to return. I sink into a chair at the table they're sharing with casseroles covered in foggy cling wrap. Across the house in the living room, my father and grandmother are in front of each other fixed in a wordless standoff about whether the casket should be open during the visitation and funeral. "But I don't know any of these people," I say. "Am I supposed to ask their names at the door?"

"Don't worry. We'll tell you," my aunt says, nudging the booklet another inch closer to my elbow.

All afternoon, my grandfather's friends and cousins drive over the big hill on the narrow road that passes in front of the house and turn in to the white gravel driveway. The women bring food, and the men bring their loud voices. My dad has a list of six names from my grandmother, and he asks those men, one by one as they arrive throughout the day, if they would do us the favor of acting as pallbearers. They are all honored, and tell my father so. I watch all of this from my perch at the kitchen table, fussing with stickers and glass dishes, drinking cup after cup of thin, instant coffee, eavesdropping as the women talk in words almost whispered. My brother stands near the door in a clump of men from town.

He doesn't know them, but they all talk like they're friends, as if my brother and not my dad was the boy who went to school and 4-H and steer shows with them, or their cousins or older brothers or fathers. They're talking about duck hunting, which my brother has been practicing for the last couple of seasons. He would actually be hunting right now, if he weren't with us for the funeral. He and his buddies go every weekend, standing in frigid flooded fields clutching their rifles and drinking beer. From the kitchen, I watch my brother tell the men about his most recent outing. His long arms point to the ceiling, and he squints one eye like he's aiming his gun. He tells about a beautiful flock of ducks that was headed his way; I imagine the huge dark V against a white sky. "But right before they're in easy range, the wind picked up. Those birds locked their wings and in one second, they were fucking gone." All of them shake their heads in silence; they sure know that story. Garrett thrusts his hands in his pockets, tilts back a little on his heels, and sighs. "So, no, we didn't bag any."

It's his phrase "locked their wings" that echoes over my roomful of women. Putting those words together is unfamiliar, but the image they conjure is exactly right—I've seen birds open out their wings straight and rigid and turn in the wind that way, like keys. This is the first time I've heard my brother make language do something surprising, and I smile because I know that he doesn't realize his words are beautiful.

On the morning of the funeral, I unzip the garment bag and lay our outfits side by side on a bed. Even just by our clothes, it's easy to see he's the larger one; the shoulders of his shirt spread wider than mine, and the cuffs of his pants nearly skim the wood floorboards. We change into our suits and stand in the kitchen. He's already wearing his new coat even though we don't have to leave for another hour. I blow on new coffee as he paces the tile floor. I can tell he's listening to the tap of his shoes on the linoleum. He rarely wears shoes like these, which is why we had to go out before driving here and buy this pair, along with the coat. His usual shoes are work boots, and all his coats are camouflage.

My mother joins us in the kitchen, picking off yellow threads of dog hair stuck to her. "You both look very nice," she says. She looks a second time at my brother, handsome and serious, and tells him she loves his new coat. Instead of finishing his lap around the kitchen, he pauses and looks down at himself to admire it. That night at the men's store, he first picked out a long, ill-fitting black one. "No, no, no," I said, and pulled this coat, the one he loves now, off a crammed rack and told him to put it on. The deep grey was a better color for his bright orange hair and yearlong sunburnt face. "Three-quarter length is nicer," I said, trading his choice for mine. "And long coats make you look like a mobster." He ignored my words—he had no idea what I was talking about—but he tried on the coat and smiled. I had guessed his size, and he fit inside it perfectly. He grinned and stared at himself in the mirror while I stood behind one of his big shoulders, only the top of my head visible, and fixed his collar.

To Bear, To Carry:
Notes on "Faggot"

. . . . .

My dear friend Tom wears eye shadow. He also often pins brooches to his shirts, just a few inches to the left of his skinny antique neckties. Both of us are instructors at the same university. On the evening after our first day of classes of this semester, we drank some wine and he told me about his morning.

"When I walked in the classroom," he started, "And before I announced I was the teacher, one of my students called me a faggot."

This had always been a fear of mine, a scenario I could imagine, and one I was actually surprised hadn't already happened. I've dealt with *faggot* for more than twenty years; I vividly remember about ten different instances of the word being used on me—and know there are more I can't as easily recall—and I doubt a similar count for any other word is possible. I've imagined Tom's classroom scenario, that is, only up to the moment when I would have to react. Tom didn't know what to do either, so he just stared at the kid—the burly, cocky guy you'd imagine, sitting in the back corner of the room of course, tilted in his chair, his arms across his chest. Tom stared and then just introduced himself to the class, wrote his name on the blackboard, and handed out copies of his syllabus.

"I can't believe that's something we really have to deal with," I said, shaking my head, and my dear friend agreed.

Then I asked him, "What were you wearing?"

"This," he said, tugging the shoulder of his cardigan, wiggling his butterfly brooch.

"I mean, not that it matters."

"Right," he said.

Later, I was bothered by my question. *What were you wearing?* Because it implied that the student might have had a good reason for saying "faggot." If Tom was dressed like one, then he was asking for it—or, if not asking, then at least his brooches and his cosmetics made the student's word understandable, explained why. And certainly it bothered me that I was trying to justify the kid's behavior. But what I most hated was this: even though I had asked my question in the unguarded comfort of close friends, the word had still tricked me. If only for a second, I was guilty of looking at my friend the same way I hated being looked at.

My earliest memory of the word comes from fourth grade, when a book titled *A Bundle of Sticks* circulated among a group of snickering classmates. Drawn in colored pencil on the cover was a sheepish boy wearing a karate uniform, his hands clasped tightly together. I didn't read the book back then, but I knew, because it was often talked about on the playground when no teachers were around that, somewhere in its pages, the boy in the uniform was called "faggot."

And actually, he was called "faggot" a couple of times; I've since tracked down the novel by Pat Mauser McCord, originally published in 1982. Ben Tyler, the main character, had a reputation as the boy who hated fighting—a fact that made him a good target for Boyd, the school bully. After the bully taunts him, forces him to eat mud at the bus-stop and kicks the Tyler family dog, Ben uses his karate self-defense classes to stand up to Boyd. But all that comes after this early scene:

The class rocked with laughter. Dennis Mathews leaned back too far and tipped his chair over. Everyone went wild, and Miss Fletcher stood up, banging on her desk with a ruler.

Boyd pointed at Ben. "Benjamin's a faggot. That's why he won't fight."

Ben felt heat rise into his face. He wanted to cover his ears and scream.

Everyone in the class pointed at him and laughed, even John who had spent a weekend with the Tylers last summer and Cindy who had his name on her love list.

Miss Fletcher then comes to Ben's rescue by demanding that Boyd tell the room the meaning of "faggot." When his definition ("It's a guy who...you know...kisses other guys and stuff") doesn't satisfy her, the teacher sends Boyd to the class dictionary. And "faggot," it turns out, surprising Boyd, Ben and the rest of the class, means "a bundle of sticks." The author doesn't describe Miss Fletcher's face in this pivotal moment, but I've imagined her smug smile, and her high-heeled shoe tapping triumphantly. As she orders Boyd back to his chair, she tells the class that any definition besides the one printed in the dictionary is slang, and therefore not appropriate.

I don't doubt that the author intended for that scene to educate her readers and disarm "faggot." Probably the bigger lesson was Ben could and should karate chop straight through his metaphorical bundle and splinter the sting of name-calling into pieces. But in my fourth grade classroom, instead of becoming a word without power, "faggot" became a word anybody could say any time without fear of retribution. Girls were called "faggot," boys were called "faggot." If a classmate cut in the lunch line, if one boy splashed another with water from the bathroom sink, if one kid threw out another in the daily kickball game at recess, all of them were faggots. And if our teacher or some other school adult overheard, the defense always pulled from back pockets was something like, "What's the big deal? All I called him was 'a bundle of sticks?'" Instead of making the word obsolete, the definition gave it cover. Objections became groundless. Because it's so simple that even a room full of nine-year-olds could figure it out: there's a difference between how a word is defined and what it really means.

No coincidence then that fourth grade was also the year when I was first called "gay." One evening after school, a classmate who lived on the next street over called me into the dark tent of trees behind our houses. Out of his slick jacket, he pulled a copy of a pornographic magazine he'd swiped from his Dad's bedroom. We crouched together in the shadows, huddling close to the edge of a creek bank, as crickets vibrated invisibly around us. On the pages he turned for the both of us, the women were naked and between their legs, quite unexpectedly, was hair. And I was so surprised by that strange secret of the female body that all I could say to my proud classmate's grin was, "Gross." But in my one word, more meaning than I had intended was revealed. The next day at school, during a group photograph of the class, I sat in the front row with the other extremely short fourth grade boy. As the teacher and the photographer directed us, telling us to sit or stand up straight, to scoot in closer, fix collars and remove hands from pockets, this boy turned to me. "You're gay, you know," he said. "You're gay because you think *Playboy* is gross."

I decide to go looking for "faggot" myself, to know what those voices are really saying when they snarl it, to uncover its violence inside. In the second edition of the *Oxford English Dictionary*, published by Clarendon Press in 1989, nearly three pages are devoted to the word and its many derivatives. The word isn't as simply defined as it was in Miss Fletcher's fictional classroom. I scribble down some of the definitions of the noun and verb forms—surprised there's a verb form at all.

noun:

1. A bundle of sticks, twigs, or small branches of trees bound together: a. for use as fuel.

2. a. With special reference to the practice of burning heretics alive, *esp.* in phrase *fire and faggot*; *to fry a faggot*, to be burnt alive; also, *to bear, carry a faggot*, as those did who renounced heresy. Hence *fig.* the punishment itself.

   b. The embroidered figure of a faggot, which heretics who had recanted were obliged to wear on their sleeve, as an emblem of what they had merited.

6. a. A term of abuse or contempt applied to a woman

   b. A (male) homosexual. *slang* (orig. and chiefly U.S.)

verb:

1. a. To make into a faggot or faggots; to bind up in or as in a faggot.

   c. To bind (persons) in couples; also, to bind hand and foot.

2. To fasten together bars or rods of iron preparatory to reheating or welding.

3. To set (a person) on the faggots preparatory to burning.

4. b. To carry or wear a faggot in token of recantation; to recant.

The tightly-packed black columns are almost dizzying. As I stand over the book, thick and worn and split-open under my eyes, just one of several volumes of *OED*, I think that more than any other, this word has probably been the biggest of my life. I've feared it; when I've heard it, it's caused the most instantaneous effect on my body, and still does—the same heat rising to my face like the character in that fourth grade book. And it can still trick me, as it did in that conversation with my friend.

So given my history with the word, I can't help but read phrases like "fry a faggot" or "to set (a person) on the faggots preparatory to burning" literally. This is what I want—the threat, for the word to *be* dangerous and not just feel that way. And certainly it's melodramatic but I suddenly can't help but consider every time I've been called "faggot," and think that person wanted me burned because of who I am. But at least in this dictionary, in these uses, burning a "faggot" doesn't mean a gay man.

Do I reach too far into the idea of burning when I wonder about the joking expression, familiar among gay people, "a flaming queen?"

On the shelf beside the *OED* is a lineup of etymological dictionaries. In one, the Cassell Dictionary of Word Histories, published by Wellington House, 1999, I find this entry for "faggot:"

> Middle English—*Faggot* was first recorded in the sense "bundle of sticks for fuel." It comes from French *fagot*, from Italian *fagotto*, based on Greek *phakelos*, "bundle." Toward the end of the 16th century, the word came to be used from dialect as an abusive term for a woman; later in the 20th century, this was applied as offensive slang in US English to a male homosexual.

Especially the French and Italian threads of origin (the Italian actually means *bassoon*) disappoint me. I wanted to see in print the connection between burning sticks and burning gay men. I pull down book after book, hunting through pages for proof. There's no denying that violence is carried inside it—centuries of burning heretics alive and "abuse" towards women—but I hoped to find actual documentation, validation of my feeling. Something like the smoking gun, instead of just some smoldering handful of sticks.

And I'm surprised that the word was first used as an insult to women, four centuries before homosexual men. I'm surprised because I've always considered "faggot" as implicitly

misogynistic, so finding this proof—however disturbing—is
heartening. To call a man "faggot" is to brand him as too
effeminate, too feminine. Which implies there's something
wrong with being feminine, especially for a man. So doesn't
hating a man because he acts like a woman suggest some hatred
for women too? Or, at the very least, doesn't it demand some
neatness to our categories? That goes there and this goes here,
let's please keep everything tidy. But the reason behind such
tidiness—why we comply and keep everything and everyone in
their separate boxes—and whether that reason is always already
ingrained in us, seems too impossible at the moment to root out.

I have only ever been called "faggot" by men, never by women.

In middle school, I stopped wearing dress shirts with that small
sewn-in loop of cloth on the back beneath the yoke and between
the shoulder blades. Boys would snag their hooked fingers on
this loop, yank it and yell, "fag tag!" Some even tried tearing it
off, as if saving you from something dangerous, like a wasp you
didn't see clinging to your back. I never told my mother why
I suddenly stopped wearing half of my wardrobe; I just said I
didn't like them anymore and hoped she didn't notice the tiny
feature the unwanted shirts had in common.

So with the single syllable *fag*, I began to fear and hate a
small inch-long strip of cloth. But why was that thing called
a "fag tag?" Because only fags would want shirts with such

unnecessary embellishments? Or because the loop is like the string, ribbon or cord bundling all those bundles of sticks? I look for the actual name of the cloth loop, but find nothing on my own. I ask a reference librarian if there is such a thing as a fashion dictionary, a garment glossary? I tell him I need to know the name of a certain part of a man's shirt. The librarian says there might be apparel guides with this kind of information—which part am I looking for?

"It's that loop of cloth on the back of a man's shirt, sewn under the yoke, in the middle."

"Well, I know the rude slang term we used in school," he says. "But that probably doesn't help you."

And it turns out there isn't any one agreed-upon term for that loop, even in apparel dictionaries, though in one clothing company's catalogs, my librarian does find "locker loop." Even so, the most common name for a nameless thing is a hateful one.

I thought of that loop of cloth when I read one of the obscure definitions of *faggot*, the one about heretics having to wear "the embroidered figure of a faggot...as an emblem of what they had merited." The small embroidered figure I imagine is cartoonish—half Boy Scout badge, half small-green-alligator sewn on polo shirts. It's a symbol simultaneously of the crime, the punishment and the confession. We'll let you go, says the little patchwork bundle, but always remember what could have happened. It's another enforcement of rules—but whose?

So it feels impossible for me to not pull together the persecution of heretics and the hatred of faggots, that is, homosexuals. Some have suggested, I discover, that because homosexuality was a crime punishable by death, homosexuals became known by the same name as the sticks that fed their fires. Burning at the stake was a common method of execution because it showed the criminals the kind of suffering they would soon endure in Hell. And it was surely spectacular, as public executions go. But this theory has been disproved because, at least in England where most of the burning of heretics took place in the fifteenth and sixteenth centuries, the period when "faggot" referred to those burning bundles, homosexuals weren't executed at the stake, they were usually hanged.

But I'm just not satisfied with the coincidence that one word has so many violent connotations over several centuries without any connections. Especially when I can string them together, however naively. Faggot is the bundle (noun), the burning of the bundle (verb), setting a heretic upon the bundle and the burning of the heretic (verbs); it's the small cloth picture of the bundle as a sign of recantation and the recantation itself; it's the action of bundling together sticks, or iron bars, or hands and feet, or people —all being tied down and into place, which makes me think again of those tidy categories, and of power, specifically the misuse of it. And the little patch of the faggot worn on the sleeve makes me think of the pink triangle patches worn on the shoulders of homosexuals when the Nazis shipped them off to camps. Which makes me think again of persecution, heretics and witches; of witches, mostly women, burned at the stake, and of *faggot* as a term of abuse for women. Persecution of homosexuals, of being hanged. Is it gratuitous, then, to see the noose wrapping around the neck as a kind of bundling? Because later in the dictionary, under "fag," I find from the fifteenth century, this definition: "a 'knot' in cloth."

More words to consider: As I write, I begin to question how I place "faggot" into my own sentences. Should it be "to call a man a faggot" or "to name a man a faggot?" The root for name comes from Latin *nomen,* which literally means "to name." Not much help. "Call" comes from late Old English *ceallian,* which comes from Old Norse *kalla,* and means "summon loudly." There's a difference, even if it's slight—naming a man a faggot means to identify him as a homosexual man, albeit by using a hostile "name;" calling a man a faggot, remembering the root, means the caller (loudly!) wants the attention of the man, even wants him closer, as in *come here, you faggot.*

When *faggot* meant "to recant" it wasn't a name, it was a command. And by recanting to stay alive, the heretic complied, guilty or not.

Maybe because I am a gay man, or maybe because I've never actually used the word against one, I realize I'm not even sure why we are called "faggot." When I try joking about the word, I always say, "Don't they think we know?" As if the reason to shout out "faggot" is because gay men need reminding— reminding that they're gay, or maybe that they're hated for it. And there's something there too about the need to categorize again, to put everybody back in the places where they supposedly belong. But. There are "gay" and "homosexual," and other words to distinguish us, after all. These are the "real" names, but ones rarely shouted out, or used as taunts like "faggot."

I understand the reason why a straight man would call another one "faggot"—which isn't to say it's any less offensive. But the suggestion is that the man in question isn't really a *man*— he's soft or weak or effeminate, etc. It's a jab at his manhood, at his gender but also his masculinity—that mysterious concoction of biology and swagger and toughness and ease that is nearly impossible to fake. I've tried. But—and I'm assuming this, that's all I can do—because the man is straight and because he knows he's not gay, he feels the word differently than I do. It's certainly insulting, and possibly threatening, but there's some essential difference in the intention that carries something more demeaning for gay men.

But isn't calling a straight man "faggot" always still an insult to gay men? Conservative writer Ann Coulter tried denying this fact in March 2007, after she implied that senator and Democratic presidential nominee John Edwards was a faggot during a speech in Washington. A few days after her remarks, on Fox News' program "Hannity and Colmes," she offered this defense: "The word I used has nothing to do with sexual preference. It isn't offensive to gays. It has nothing to do with gays. It is a schoolyard taunt meaning 'wuss.' And unless you're telling me that John Edwards is gay, it was not applied to a gay person." She's right on only one point—she didn't call John Edwards "gay." Calling him "a homosexual" would have been toothless. But with his $400 haircuts, bright smile and lovely moisturized skin, calling Edwards "faggot" actually bites—which is why the story had so much traction in the media in the days following the slur. Because she's not saying that John Edwards is sexually attracted to men; she's saying he *passes* for a man sexually attracted to men—and also implying such slippage disqualifies him from politics. We all know he's married but that doesn't make him a *man*, and only a man can be president. And yes, it is a schoolyard taunt, but not one that simply means "wuss," and that was clear in fourth grade. What's also clear is calling John Edwards "faggot" is perceived as an insult to him because it's an insult to gay men—straight men don't just laugh it off; they fight back because a faggot is someone already pushed aside and trivialized. Even in *A Bundle of Sticks* when our hero Ben finally stands up to the bully, he defends himself by asking, "How can I have a girlfriend...if I'm supposed to be a faggot?" But defending yourself against the taunt when you're actually gay doesn't come with any such reliable escape hatch.

We learn our names only by being called them.

I was most recently called "faggot" two months ago. I was riding my bike in my mid-western college town, late at night as the bars were emptying. While I pedaled through an intersection, a young guy, probably a student like one of my students, called the word out to me. I just kept riding. I've never found a good enough comeback. There really isn't an argument because according to the dictionary, it's true—I am gay, so yes, I am a faggot.

There's something else going on underneath that I wish I could ignore. Once, as a very closeted undergraduate, I was at a party with my two closest friends, a straight woman and a gay man. The party was crowded, and most of the men there were straight. In those years, when I was being honest with myself, I knew I was gay, but I was trying desperately not to be—bargaining with God every night in prayer to help me stop thinking *that way* about men, and occasionally even dating women. Before the party, we had some drinks and, after arriving, did shots together in the kitchen of the too-hot house. As we wiped our tingling lips and shook off our quick jolts of vodka, I looked across the living room and a single face stood out.

He was the best combination possible of pretty boy and those clichéd chiseled features of tall, dark and handsome.

Except he wasn't that tall—he was about my height with the veiny, tight skin of a runner shown off by rolled-up sleeves. Lovely clean-shaven cheeks, short brown hair, a jawline as sharp and solid as a table's edge and big, soft eyes. I couldn't stop staring.

And in my drunkenness, I forgot myself, and kept staring. I forgot I was pretending I wasn't gay, and forgot too that not all men appreciated adoration from other men, confused, innocent or otherwise. After a couple more hours of drinking and gazing, on our way out the front door, stumbling behind my two friends, we passed this man, and as I looped my eyes toward him to snag one final glance, he leaned in a few inches from my face, and sneered, "Faggot."

No one heard it but me. My friends and I walked outside and got halfway to the car before I said anything. "Some guy just called me a 'faggot,'" I said, nearly chuckling. "What?" asked my gay friend. I repeated, and he was incensed, certainly fueled by his own relationship with the word.

"Who?" he asked.

I shrugged. "Some guy by the door."

He marched back toward the party, leaving me and my other friend standing in the street. "It's not a big deal!" I called out, but he kept going. Of course I'd left out the most important piece of the truth. And it makes me wonder if there are moments when gay men might actually deserve scorn—at that party, leering at an obviously straight man, was I being a faggot?

If I've known since fourth grade that what is intended by the word is not how it's defined, then why does it still burn? There must be violence and hatred carried in it, even if I can't locate the satisfying, definitive connection on paper. If it isn't to voice a desire to destroy us, then why call gay men "faggots?"

But even after what I've uncovered, I'm unsettled because words aren't simply good or evil. Shouldn't I feel inspired because as a writer I need words to be beautiful, and even powerful, as well as ugly and dangerous? Shouldn't I of all people know that a word's potential for comfort or harm rests in how it is used? So if the letters themselves are innocent, if the meaning isn't in the word, or just in the word, then it's us carrying around those threats and violence. Like a recanting heretic, I'm the one complying with the word's hatred, and allowing it to bear down on me—the way it surely will until I harden myself against hearing it. Such a revelation is both startling and obvious, and I'm stuck there, bound up in that original trick of the word: When I wince at its sting, I share its intention—if only for a second.

The Goldfish History

· · · · ·

Hope is a goldfish in a plastic bag of water: the weight of the bag in your hands, how the cold bundle must be cradled to prevent jostling the poor creature inside; the transparency of the bag, how white your hands look through the water, the plastic wrinkles that gather around the ridges of your fingers; the goldfish itself, which isn't really gold, or just gold—it bobs around and if you're driving home from the fish store, riding beside your roommate, there's the inevitable moment when the fish will ease into his surroundings, float to the bottom of the bag resting in the warm palm of your hand, and as the car rounds a curve, you feel the flutter of his translucent tail against your skin through the plastic.

This goldfish meant hope because we hoped the one in our bag would be one to survive. Not just three weeks, but years, the way goldfish are supposed to. We hoped it wasn't one with that goldfish parasite called "Ich," short for "Ichtyopthirius" but everyone thinks is "Ick" because it's a parasite, which is gross. We hoped we wouldn't have to flush the fish in a few days if we found him with his pale belly turned toward the ceiling of the water. We hoped that buying all this fish stuff wasn't wasting our money.

But also because of the delicacy involved—floating the bag in the new bowl for an hour to allow the fish to adjust temperatures, treating our Chicago tap water with mysterious chemical drops—the goldfish was hope: this fragile thing who was dependent on us and our care, silent and colorful and ours to name.

I can't remember if it was my roommate Kim or me who first thought of getting a goldfish. And I can't remember who suggested his name—Rufus—though it was probably me. After Rufus Wainwright, our favorite singer at the time, and the man I called my boyfriend because I had the biggest and most hopeless of crushes on him, and because I didn't have an actual boyfriend. I used to say that Rufus the man brought me more pleasure than any of the men I'd actually dated. His picture was taped to the refrigerator door, I owned all his albums, went to every nearby performance—that kind of thing. Rufus the fish was always supposed to have a companion, another fish that we planned to name after a cute actor from some TV show, whose name I can't remember, but we never made it back to the fish store.

So on a bright Sunday afternoon in Chicago in March, Kim and I ripped open a sack of brown gravel and dumped an inch in Rufus's new glass bowl. The guy at the fish store had steered us away from pointy plastic seaweed and gave us instead a clipping of some soft green vine—an actual plant—that coiled through the water like a spiral staircase. We also got a chunk of driftwood instead of one of those pink plastic castles or bubbling sunken treasure chests. The moment we untied the watery sack and poured Rufus into his bowl, we stared at him swimming around, and it felt good, because it was something we could share, and something that we needed.

Kim and I had been best friends for five years, since our freshman year of college. After I graduated a year ahead of her, I moved to Chicago. A year after that move, one weekend when she was visiting, I came out to her—she was the first person to ever hear me say, "I am gay." When I told her, we were standing in a gay bar. In the *women's* restroom of the gay bar—a bar we'd been to several times before that night. In this private bathroom, giant mirrors stood all around us with their backs against the walls; as I told Kim what I had to tell her, I watched our dim and infinite reflections do exactly what we were doing. Before finally speaking those words, I had known I was gay but wasn't ready to admit it. Before that, I knew I was gay but made myself date girls because I didn't want to be. Before that, for almost all of my teenage years, I thought I might be gay and was afraid so I prayed every night for it to be taken away. And before that, I didn't know I was gay, but I knew I was different, and I didn't want to be that either.

At the time, when I had to offer a reason for picking up and moving to Chicago with some savings, my car and two splitting boxes crammed too full of books, I said I wanted to live in a big city. Only later would I see it more precisely as looking for a place big enough to get lost in, with space to figure out if I wanted to allow myself to be honest. Coming from the Missouri suburbs, Chicago felt limitless—the way it probably feels for any twenty-two-year-old looking for something. Even so, those possibilities felt private and singular, like finding something everybody else had overlooked—a quarter waiting and shining right there on the sidewalk.

"Oh my God," was Kim's reaction in that bathroom, dance floor music thumping through the door. Even in a gay bar, the news that your best friend is gay can come as a surprise. A cigarette burned between her fingers, she leaned against the tiled counter. Her round face turned pink. "Why didn't you ever tell me before?"

"I haven't been keeping it from you," I said. "I'm still figuring it out myself."

Despite all evidence to the contrary—because I'd spent so long denying I was gay, she believed me because that was her job. *If I could tell anyone I could tell her* was the thinking, and not just because she was my best friend, but because she was also a friend to all gay men, it seemed. *Every* other man she knew was gay. She learned how to smoke, drink, dance and make fake ID's from the gay hustlers she'd hung out with since high school.

Besides the surprise she felt, she also knew that I needed

her. So twenty days later, she drove 300 miles to Chicago with her own car full of boxes, piled them on the floor of my studio, and we waited together for the lease to begin at our new two-bedroom apartment.

At the beginning, Rufus hated me. He hid whenever I walked in the front door, darting off and hovering behind those heavy seaweed leaves. It didn't even seem possible to hide in a goldfish bowl—a place where everything is out in the open—but he found the way. Though he never hid from Kim. "Even my goldfish doesn't want to look at me," I'd complain, slumping next to her on the sofa, mostly joking. She was single too, and we spent our entire weekends drinking whiskey, searching for men.

"Maybe it's your voice," she said. We would have been uncorking red wine, a movie playing on TV though we'd talk through the whole thing, eating something covered in cheese.

"I don't think goldfish have ears."

"Well, it's just your presence then. You probably make him nervous." And with my photocopied, spreadsheet grocery lists, meal calendars and rules about ashtrays and coasters, I made more than just Rufus nervous. You know you live in a smothering routine when an idea like, "Let's get a goldfish!" sounds exciting.

Every time he hid, I thought about his view of things from in there. Even if he did have ears, I imagined his bowl as completely silent—scary and muffled like sitting at the bottom

of a swimming pool. And how strange to see *us* in his water—
which must have looked to him the same as the glass that held
it, which also must have looked the same as the air surrounding
it, the air that Kim and I moved through. Did he think all of us
were underwater, part of the same big thing? There was probably
clear separation, an *in here* and *out there* but there wasn't any
visible boundary—sort of an edge to feel but never see.

The only time he didn't hide from me was in the morning
when I fed him, and it was my favorite time to watch him. After
opening the curtains in the front window, I uncapped the small
can of fish food and pinched some between my fingers. I'd let
them spring open over the bowl and watch the clump of flakes
fall; yellow, brown and orange, the thin bits of food exploded
over the surface, covering the whole bare face of the water as he
ascended. His white mouth closed over the bits, his orange body
wiggling and twisting as the food soaked around him, and sank.

Every Friday night, Kim and I went to our bar, the one where
I came out, and drank and danced. Every Friday night. The
bouncer hugged Kim at the door whenever we arrived. I had
a crush on the guy named Joe who checked coats, whom we
called Coat Check Joe, and every week, she and I shared in the
anticipation of my seeing him again. He didn't know my name
but he pretended he was excited and kissed my cheek with
his whiskery face, and that was all it took to love him. Being

regulars there, as well as at our Thursday and Saturday places, made us feel as though we belonged to something.

But being such regular regulars also got boring, and even we, roommates and best friends since college, would run out of things to talk about. That's what happened one Friday night in April, about a month after the arrival of Rufus. In the dark back room with the pool table, we sat side by side on a bench, rattling ice in empty glasses.

"What should we do tomorrow?" one of us asked.

The other one shrugged. "I don't know."

We sat, looked at people, rattled ice again, tipped back glasses for one more watery sip, looked around again, pointed at someone's ugly shirt, sighed.

"Another drink?" I said, hopping up.

"Sure."

I bumped my way through the crowd of men. It had been ten months since I'd come out of the closet, and I'd dated, but nothing serious. Sometimes I felt too immature to date. Because I'd spent my teenage years pretending and denying, I'd missed out on melodrama and note-passing, first kisses with braces and school dance jealousies. So now I was 23 and unable to talk to attractive men without blushing, giggling, or touching my face a lot and looking at the floor. The only way I ever met men was because Kim could talk to anyone, and often did.

The bartender made two whiskey and cokes without me

even ordering, and I threw down exact change. As I headed back to Kim, I saw him: about my height with uncombed dark hair, huge brown eyes and a lopsided smile, wearing a red and white striped Polo shirt. One thin hand was lifted, and it pushed back the front of his hair as if he posed for something. He was talking to a man next to him, and I was glad because I was very obviously staring. It was love at first sight, though I wouldn't ever tell him.

"I just saw the cutest guy," I said, when I handed Kim her drink. "He looks like Rufus Wainwright." I sat and sipped and thought. "Oh my God. What if it *is* Rufus Wainwright?"

"Rufus Wainwright is not at this bar," she said, stirring.

Suddenly this dream guy was walking toward us, the way it's supposed to happen in love stories. Coincidentally, his roommate was a guy we'd talked to a few weeks before, so they both came up, and the beautiful one sat beside me. He and his roommate were also best friends and had also just moved to Chicago, and we were all the same age. His name was Geoffrey, spelled the cute way.

"Do you know who Rufus Wainwright is?" I asked him.

"No," he said.

"Well, he's this singer I like, I named my goldfish after him. You look like him. Or he looks like you."

"You have a goldfish?"

"Yeah. Well, it's ours," I said, swinging my head toward Kim, who was talking to the roommate. "Ours together."

A month later, Geoffrey told Kim that he liked me, and she told me. Then I told him that I liked him back, and we started dating. It seemed perfect, maybe even fateful—dating a man who looked like a man I loved enough to give his name to a fish. A couple of years later, I would tell Geoffrey how that first memory was so embedded in my head that it was as though him standing there with his hand on his hair was a photograph I could hold up whenever I wanted. I knew right where he was in the bar, I told him, what he was wearing, and doing.

"I don't remember any of that," he said. "What shirt did I have on?"

"The white one with the red stripes. And the collar. You never wear it anymore."

He thought a minute. "I've never owned a shirt like that."

From the beginning, Rufus liked Geoffrey, who liked Rufus, always calling the fish by his own nickname, "Pretty" while he would stand by the glass bowl and dip his fingertips just inside the water. Rufus climbed to the top and nibbled.

"Look. He's kissing my fingers," Geoffrey said.

"Because he thinks it's food," I said.

"No, it's kissing."

After only a few weeks, I rarely slept alone. Geoffrey slept in my bed half the time in the apartment I shared with Kim, and the other half, we slept in his bed across town. Kim was supposed to remember to feed Rufus on those mornings, but rarely did. When Geoffrey and I slept, I clung to him the way you do only early in love when the comfort of that other body is better than the comfort of actually sleeping. Later, I would announce a "no touching" rule because living, breathing skin against my skin kept me awake. But that was later. In those touching-and-sleeping days, after a few weeks, I knew this was the first time I would be in love.

Kim started watching TV more often, and grocery shopping and making dinner alone, and spending nights on her own at the laundromat because I did laundry in Geoffrey's neighborhood. She talked long-distance to friends in other cities, and stuffed unpaid bills into a shoebox she kept under her bed. When Geoffrey slept over, in the morning when all of us had to get ready for work in that small, foggy bathroom, there was a lot of door slamming.

One weekend, Geoffrey was out of town and Kim and I watched movies in our apartment and drank whiskey. We made egg rolls, played board games, painted our toenails. I waited for one of us to say, "This is just like old times." We kept drinking whiskey, and talking and snacking, and then she said that as close as we were, there was something that she'd never told me.

"What?" I said. My spine was a hard straight line on the couch, she was perched on a nest of pillows on the carpet in front of me, legs crossed. Water filled to her eye rims.

"If you don't know, then I don't want to tell you."

"What are you talking about?" I kept on asking until our

glasses were empty and she got up to make refills. The next morning she said, "I don't remember that at all." And though I might have guessed what she wanted to tell me but couldn't let herself, it was easier to do what she was doing, and forget. It was in those days that I thought the size of a goldfish was determined by the size of the bowl it lived in. I said to Kim, Geoffrey, and anyone else that Rufus knew how much to grow, that somehow a goldfish's body only grew as large as their vessel could contain. I'd later learn that the size of goldfish is determined instead by the surface area of the water, by how much water is exposed to the air. I'd also find out that a group of goldfish is known as a troubling.

Months later, when I got home from work one evening, Kim and Geoffrey sat on the front porch smoking, sharing an ashtray. She'd been waiting for me so she could tell us something. "So I've made a decision," she announced. "I'm moving back to Missouri." I thought she meant at the end of the school year; she was a teacher. "I'm going next week," she said. That day, she'd turned in a letter of resignation to her principal; her grandmother had died and she was shouldered with taking care of her frail grandpa, now alone. It was a lie.

"Oh," I said. I didn't ask why.

She spent the next couple of days packing, taking only what she could fit in her car—the same way we'd both arrived to the city she was now leaving. Her suitcase would be stuffed so full of clothes that she'd call me into her room to help her zip it. I kneed the bulk down, pulled together the rows of teeth, and yanked on the slippery key. She took some of her board games, and some of her kitchen stuff and some of her CDs, the important ones she'd need for the seven-hour drive, some of her movies and books. The rest, she said, would have to wait until later. She didn't ask about Rufus, and I hoped she wouldn't because I didn't want her to take him. He was our fish but he should stay here, in this apartment in Chicago.

But before the packing, on the night of her porch announcement, the three of us made dinner, drank wine, and watched something boring on TV. We didn't talk about anything. Then we went to bed, Kim to her room, Geoffrey and me to mine. In the dark, I slid under the blankets and fell on him, my mouth open over the arch of his collarbone, and I sobbed silently so she wouldn't hear me through our thin common wall. "Am I a bad friend? What did I do?" I whispered over and over, and he held me. A month and a half later he moved in. We bought a new green sofa, a lamp, a two-gallon glass jar for Rufus to replace his small round bowl, and a $15 sack of polished river stones to tile his floor instead of his brown gravel. I put the old bowl in a closet and eventually, Geoffrey carried it out to the alley. We didn't know what else to do with it; a goldfish bowl is one of those things that you don't ever need more than one of.

———

If Rufus grew in his new jar, I didn't notice. Because as soon as we poured him in from his former bowl, he simply looked bigger—a trick of the water and the roundness of glass. Then at certain points in his swimming along the curve of the jar, he could actually disappear. It was as if he could come and go as he wanted, and when I'd look across the room, and see the empty jar, I'd panic until he slowly emerged, like a ghost walking out of a wall. Geoffrey still let him kiss his fingers, and still called him "Pretty," and I still fed him in the morning—a plop of flakes in the center of his air circle, now much larger, while I pulled open the curtains to watch his sheer tail ripple and wave in the sun.

Geoffrey and I kept buying things for the apartment, went on vacations, joined a gym with a "partner" discount, took a kickboxing class, and neatly printed each other's names in the Emergency Contact boxes of official forms. We bought a fireproof box for our birth certificates, social security cards and passports, and hid them under our bed. Kim called sometimes and I had to ask her to send checks for leftover bills, and she got angry. But everything felt as though it was out in the open now, there was no place or need anymore to hide because I didn't have to manage myself between she and Geoffrey. Everything felt easier.

A month or so later, I was in bed, pillows stuffed behind my back, and I turned a new page in my journal to find scribbles across the ruled lines. Geoffrey had written *She's in love with you, you know* in purposeful blue ink—I only ever wrote in black.

He'd chosen a page at random months before and I was just reaching it. I glared at him, sleeping beside me, his shoulder warm against my thigh. More than just the fact that he'd been snooping around my most private sentences, I hated that he'd written down what none of us had ever spoken. Here were the two biggest secrets I knew of—the one about how Kim really felt about me and the one about how I didn't know. But instead of waking him and calling him names like Passive-Aggressive, I just wrote around his words.

Soon after, one morning, I pulled open the curtains, looked at the line of sun cutting across Rufus's jar, and he was on the rocks, lying on his side. Between his fins and tail, there was now a crimp, and he was folded in half like a Christmas card. Pushing back my shirtsleeve, I reached through his water, my arm turning white, to nudge him. He flipped his tail, wobbled upside down and swam in weird directions as though he were caught in a current. He wasn't dead.

"What's wrong with him?" Geoffrey asked, standing at the jar in his underwear because I'd dragged him out of bed.

"He's probably got some disease contracted from dirty fingers," I said.

"Yeah, that's it," he said, sliding his feet back to our bed. "He'll be fine."

I called the fish store anyway, listed symptoms, described the wobbling and weird drifting, the tail crimp. A teenage voice listened, then asked, "Do you feed the fish dry flake food?"

"Well, yes."

"OK. So the fish is constipated."

"But it's *fish* food. What do you feed fish if not fish food?" I said.

"That's easy." From now on, every morning, or even better, every other morning, Rufus should be fed a single thawed, peeled, crushed green pea.

After all the bills were paid, and she returned to Chicago once more to pick up the rest of her stuff, I didn't talk to Kim for a long time. I ignored her e-mails. I didn't return her calls. I felt as though there wasn't enough space in my brain or heart to fit the trouble between us. There, in her own city, she lived a life and, at least for that time being, I liked how far away it was from Geoffrey's and mine.

With his new green pea diet, Rufus swam straight and upright again, but his crimp remained, as though he were made of pie dough and had been squished too tightly between fingers. I hated the slimy mess of pea-feeding, so Geoffrey took over. But every morning after I slid apart the curtains, I still watched Rufus turn in the yellow light while I drank my coffee.

More vacations, more new furniture. Geoffrey got a new job, I got promoted. We re-painted the bathroom. The fish store was re-sided in dark blue vinyl, an aquatic reference certainly, but then it went out of business and became a mattress store— just a blue mattress store. Whole years went by. One evening

Geoffrey and I met for dinner at the chicken kabob place; I'd been away from home all day, he'd just come from there. As he walked through the glass door, I saw that he had something to tell me right there on his face.

"Rufus is sick again," he said, sliding into our booth.

"What's wrong with him?"

"That same thing. He's swimming on his side like he can't get his balance. He was laying on the rocks when I got home."

"Did you feed him this morning?"

"Yes," he said, rolling his eyes.

I remembered that the pet store guy had said toxins could build up in the water if you didn't have a filter (we didn't) or didn't clean out the jar often enough (we hadn't). "What time is it?" I said, wrenching his wrist so I could read his watch.

"Rufus will be fine," he said, pulling his arm from my hand. "I mean, he's not *fine*, but he'll be fine until we get home."

"I wish they'd hurry up with the food."

After we ate, in the parking lot, we got in our separate cars, and I started home. I ran a red light and swerved in front of an old woman trying to make a right turn. I couldn't wait for her. And even as I stormed through Chicago traffic, cursing every stoplight that snared me, I knew how ridiculous I'd sound to the cop I was convinced would eventually handcuff me for reckless driving. "I have to get home right way, Officer, it's an emergency—my goldfish is dying." Something about keeping Rufus alive was more urgent than just the fact that he would be dead.

Goldfish have a reputation for dying. When I told people I'd had a goldfish four, then five, then six years and counting, they would be impressed—with Rufus or me, I wasn't sure. It seemed uncommon to have a goldfish so long, even if the possible lifespan is around twenty years. Goldfish also have a reputation for being disposable. If it dies, you get another one. The pet store tanks are full of hundreds and maybe even thousands of them, glittering and tightly packed together like sewn sequins. Drunk kids used to swallow them as a dare because presumably no one would miss a few dozen, so why not? It might be said that goldfish aren't usually important.

On the day we bought him, Kim and I stood in front of that crammed glittering tank at the fish store, and I kept my eye on Rufus as the guy dunked his green net in again and again, creating mayhem in the water, each time scooping up the wrong one. "No, that's not him." I pointed to Rufus, and waited. I can't say what it was that Rufus had that the other fish didn't, though his throat was marked distinctively in silvery white. But I knew which one I wanted, the only one I wanted—fish love at first sight.

Once Rufus was sick, and he was staying sick, I realized that he stood for a lot —hope, my friendship with Kim, its failure, my love with Geoffrey, its growth. Because why else would I be so upset over the dying of this silent orange fish? And it didn't matter how silly it felt to be worried. Mornings changed: I approached his bowl carrying my cup of coffee as well as the anxiety that I would find him dead. And it was all made worse by the idea that I didn't know what to do for him. Taking him to a veterinarian or a fish doctor was hopeless because I already knew what I'd hear. *Well, it is just a goldfish.*

Kim and I didn't speak for almost two years. And then she came back to Chicago to visit some mutual friends, and she wanted to see me. At a small party, she and I sat on our friends' back porch, knees nearly touching. It was strange how easy it was to talk, and how smoothed out our history felt because it was history. She was doing well in her city, Geoffrey and I were too, in ours. After enough glasses of wine, we told each other we were sorry for what happened, for how she'd left. I wanted to tell her that I knew I hadn't been very fair, that for so many years I'd made her the stand-in for the companion I wouldn't let myself have, until that companion came along. And probably my needing her so transparently let Kim hope for something more than just friendship between us—even if it didn't make much sense for her to keep that hope around. But I would never ask if that was true. Because for all the things we said, we allowed each other not to say all the things we might have.

"Oh," Kim asked, after so much serious talk. "How's Rufus?"

I smiled. "He's fine. He eats peas now, but he's still with us."

"I can't believe that," she said, shaking her head. "That's amazing he's still alive."

A year later, she visited Chicago again, and that time, she stayed with Geoffrey and me in the apartment that she and I had once shared, sleeping in her former bedroom. After she flopped down her suitcases, I took her on a short tour of the rooms we'd repainted, the green kitchen where we'd stripped off the ugly floral wallpaper, the bathroom now a color named "stone." "I'm sorry. I can't remember what it looked like before," she said.

It was the reaction I'd anticipated. "How is that possible? You *lived* here," I said, and she shrugged, and we laughed at how well we still knew each other.

She and Geoffrey and I stood in the dining room, in front of Rufus's new jar that wasn't new anymore with his smooth river stones, and she poked her fingertip in the water and drew ripples across the surface as Rufus fluttered. The dining room walls were now gorgeous deep orange that matched him—my favorite color; Geoffrey had painted the room by himself as a surprise for me. The next day was Friday, and I took the day off to go shopping with Kim. It was also my and Geoffrey's sixth anniversary.

He got home from work a little after five, and called my cell phone as Kim and I sat exhausted in rush-hour traffic, weakly singing songs in a fierce sunset. "I have bad news," he said. "Rufus died."

"Oh," I said, in a sad enough note that Kim knew even without hearing his words.

"Did Rufus die?" she whispered as Geoffrey continued talking in my ear. I nodded.

By the time we returned to the apartment, Geoffrey had drained and scrubbed out Rufus's jar. The stones were piled in the sink, dark and glistening with soap bubbles. Rufus lay on a tiny white bed of folded paper towels. His mercurial eyes had already turned black.

"I think we should bury him," one of us said.

As he dried in the air and the luster of his scales dulled, all the colors I'd always noticed in his body seemed to disappear, and I wondered if I had always imagined the green, blue, red and grey. Geoffrey bundled the paper towel around him and I closed it with a strip of tape. We were going to bury him in the back yard.

"Make him a headstone," Geoffrey said because he knew I would want to do it. He pulled a flat-sided stone from the heap in the sink.

I patted it dry and wrote Rufus's name across it in permanent marker. "Wait," I said, and ran across the kitchen to the bedroom. On my knees, I dug under our bed for the journal I was writing in the year Kim and I bought Rufus. "I want to put his dates on the stone," I called out. I knew it had been March, and I thought it was early in the month and almost certainly a weekend, probably Sunday. As I flipped through pages, passing all those old recorded days, I skimmed for his name. Kim and I buying a pet would have been a big enough event to write down. And I *remembered* writing it down, but it wasn't there. I checked February, turning page after page, searching for his name or any word that would signal the story of his coming. I checked January, though I knew it would have been too early; April was too late because in April we knew Geoffrey. "What are you doing?" he said, from the kitchen. They were waiting, so I just wrote down his lifespan in years, wondering what sense I could make of any of this if I couldn't get my memory to match the facts.

We stood in the back yard. Under unruly lilac branches showing off new blooms, I dug out a hole with a hand trowel. "What do we say?" Geoffrey asked, dropping the white packet in, covering it with dirt, and tamping down the stone on top.

"I don't know," I said, and we all stared at the rock.

Kim sighed. "To Rufus. A great fish. We love you."

For so long, even though we knew he was sick, it seemed as though Rufus might just go on living the way he was. He survived one day with his tail crimp, so he'd always survive the next. But there we were. I wanted to say something about how uncanny it was that he'd died *that* day, on my anniversary with Geoffrey, how our relationship had always been as old as he was, and how it was also the weekend that Kim was back in the apartment for the first time in years, several of which had passed in silence. And that I was sorry for what I had hoped for the three of us back then—for everybody to contain their feelings, for nothing to ever change.

———

A year later, when Geoffrey and I finally moved from that apartment to another state, we took Rufus's old stones with us. I'd always planned to do something with them, and still thought I would, so we packed them into a shoebox stuffed with wads of newspaper. At our new house, on the day we moved in, Geoffrey unpacked the stones, and piled them in the front flowerbed in the spot under the mailbox. He cleared out the weeds, and the smooth dark rocks sat there like the marker of something. We unpacked everything else and made the stuff of our life fit this new place. That first night, we fell into our same bed in our different room, and when I switched off the lamp, I said, "Look." On the ceiling was a sky of glow-in-the-dark stars, leftovers. "Wow," he said, and we kissed, and slept.

Months later, it was somehow over between us, and I lived in the house alone and he moved to his own city, and we had crossed through each other's names in those Emergency Contact boxes. And I spent a lot of time thinking about how you can be sure of something and still always be wrong. In the front flowerbed, the weeds grew and I didn't keep up with them and eventually, I noticed they were taller than Rufus' pile and I just let them go. I decided then that I would leave his stones there, even when I moved from the house to any future place. I like imagining someone pulling weeds one day, revealing the pile of them again, and this person thinking the stones odd and beautiful without having any idea of what they really mean.

Things I Will Want to Tell You on Our First Date but Won't

. . . . .

That I've had a crush on you for a long time. That besides your name, I don't actually know you. That the first time I saw you I didn't think you were as cute as I think you are now, and this is a good sign. That the first time I saw you, I just thought you looked nice, and I thought if we went on a date, we'd probably have a nice time. That I also thought, He could be one who gets me over my ex. That I even thought, He could be *the* one, but not like the other one, my ex, who I used to think was *the* one—until he broke up with me, and then became just the last one. That I don't understand how you can think you're with *the* one only to find out later you are not. That I've Googled you.

That, like a sixth-grade girl with a pink notebook, I've thought about how our names go together. That, unlike the girl with the notebook, I've never written our names next to each other to see how they look, though I've considered it. That I am thankful your name isn't the same as mine, which is probably the biggest disadvantage gay people have in dating—the chance of dating someone who has your name. That I could never, never date someone with my name. That I think this is so creepy, I can't think of a man perfect enough to be the exception to this rule. That I'm also thankful my name isn't Michael or something as hopelessly common because then my already shallow dating pool would be suddenly drained. That in high school when I was obsessed with 1960s Warren Beatty movies, I wanted to change my name to Warren, which is embarrassing to admit but would have helped with this no-same-name policy because I've never actually met a Warren.

That our first date will be my first date in eight years, and counting. That our first date will be my first first date since my first date with my ex. That I don't know what to do on first dates. That my first date with my ex is a blur because I was thinking, This is my first date with this guy I like so much! It's happening right now! the whole time so I won't have much to compare our date to. That I didn't date much before my ex and then when he came along, we were together for eight years. That other than a two-week thing with this too-beautiful and too-young guy whose idea of dating was to stop by my house whenever he wanted to make out with me on my sofa and then leave about an hour later, I haven't dated since my ex and I broke up a year ago.

That for a long time after my ex broke up with me, I thought I was fine because I always think I'm fine. That I'd pretended I was fine all of spring and summer until one afternoon I was talking to him on the phone. He and I are trying to be friends, which is sometimes hard because when I first saw him, I didn't want to be his friend, I wanted to be his boyfriend. That I don't want to be his boyfriend anymore, though this hasn't always been true since the break-up. That when we were talking on the phone and he finally told me the name of his new boyfriend, even though I already knew he was dating someone else and thought it was way too soon for him to be doing so, it was hearing the man's name. That we talked a bit more and then he had to go and it wasn't until I tried to aim my fingertip at the END on my cell phone that I noticed my hands were shaking. That his new boyfriend's name is not Warren or Michael or the same as mine.

That I wasn't fine. That I had been ignoring how non-fine I was. For example, I had chosen not to notice the fact that I hadn't really slept since he broke up with me. And if I ever slept, I'd wake in the dark as if out of a nightmare, breathless, my heart knocking hard like an angry landlord. And my hands didn't only vibrate after hearing the names of new boyfriends—they shook all the time. My stomach was stuck on simmer, and all I ever ate were spoonfuls of peanut butter *and* jelly straight out of the jar. That I was usually wearing only underwear when I ate these spoonfuls, and afterwards, I'd lie down in the middle of the afternoon and take long naps on the hardwood floor and wake up sweating. That I hated turning so easily into the jilted sad-sack cliché. That I finally understood the point of clichés—they feel comfortable.

That I should have known something was wrong because I was writing a lot of break-up poetry. That when I searched for "gay break up" books at Amazon.com, the first result was *Cowboys: Erotic Tales.*

That I saw a therapist, another cliché, which felt comfortable. That when my therapist said, "Why don't you start at the beginning?" before I could make the first syllable of the first word, which was going to be something simple like, "Okay," my voice came undone, and I started crying. That I hate crying in front of people, especially men. That crying in front of him felt embarrassing but also oddly consoling *because* he was a man. That once I started, I couldn't stop talking and crying, and telling the whole story from the beginning while my therapist took notes on a clipboard. That once I stopped, he looked at his scribbles and said, "I'm just doing the math here, but was this your first boyfriend, your first significant relationship?" and I said, "Yes." That my therapist leaned deep in his chair as his eyes turned to the ceiling and his head tilted back, and he said, with a big open mouth, "Ah."

That I hate when I tell people we were together for eight years and now we're not, and they put their hand on my shoulder and say, "Oh I'm so sorry," as if somebody died. That sometimes it feels like somebody died. That even my therapist said, "What you need to do is mourn the loss, to give yourself permission to grieve for the relationship." That months later, I was teaching a poem about death and grief to a room full of nineteen year olds, and I asked, "So how do we bring an end to mourning?" and one of my students said, "Eat lunch." That I think this kid should be my therapist. That I never say the word, "dumped." That I always say it was my ex's decision.

That if he hadn't broken up with me, I would have stayed with him forever.

That when I see you, I don't know what to do with my body. That when I see you, my eyes just want to stay there looking at your face. That whenever you see me looking at you, I have to look away because of the not knowing what to do with my body. That I don't know how to walk across rooms and talk to strangers, especially male strangers who are cute, and who have seen me look at them and then look away, even if I think they want me to. That I also don't know how to arrange my body to look like someone who wants the cute male stranger across the room to walk over. That the first time I crossed the room to talk to a cute stranger, and tried to hand him a small square of paper on which I'd written my phone number, he didn't want it and said so in a nice enough way, but I still walked off vowing never to do that again. That I have never done that again. That I will never do that again.

That I realized my ex breaking up with me changed the way I thought about my body, which is why I don't know what to do with it when you look. That I once imagined what I must look like to you, and from this point-of-view, I understood I needed new jeans and to start doing sit-ups. Also, a haircut. That I stood on tiptoes in front of my medicine cabinet mirror, shirt off, and actually said to the dog, "I *really* have to start doing sit-ups," and when she didn't know what I meant, I realized how much I talk to the dog. That she used to be our dog and now she's just my dog.

That my body actually feels different now, maybe even unfamiliar, as though it was gone eight years and suddenly returned, like when a friend borrows a book for so long that when you finally get it back, you forgot you ever owned it. That it's because he knew my body better than any other man, and he told me he loved it while overlooking its certain flaws, and now that he's left, I feel as though I don't only have to meet a whole new man but I also have to convince him to think the same way about my body. And on top of it, I should probably like him back. That one of the first things I said to my ex when he broke up with me was, "I can't believe you're making me have to date again."

That other than the too-young and too-beautiful two-week guy, and a stranger who grabbed me from behind in a public restroom, no man has touched me since my ex.

That I think you know you have a crush when the man you already think is cute is always cuter than you remembered each time you come across him in your day, and it's something about seeing him move around in the world which makes him cuter, not just his face. That sometimes I imagine what we'll do on a quiet Saturday afternoon, like get to-go cups of tea and take the dog to the forest preserve and hook our index fingers together and walk the trails swinging arms, half-mocking couples that walk swinging arms and half-enjoying the swinging of arms. Or even if the sun is out and shining, we can lie on the bed, each of us reading separate books while sharing a bag of candy and not caring that we're wasting good weather because we'll both agree that books are better than anything. That small thoughts of you—even though I don't know you—sometimes interrupt what I'm doing; like if I'm stirring a pot of soup, I'll wonder if you love tomatoes as much as me. Little things like that. That I try to assume this is what everyone does when they think about a crush though I've never confirmed this. That I do not want to confirm this.

That part of the weirdness I feel when you look at me is the sensation of having a crush, and it's because I haven't been on a first date in so long that I've forgotten this feeling. That I wonder if you can keep having a crush on a man you know and love.

That the truth is, even though I thought my ex and I were mostly happy, or happy enough, I could still always imagine loving another man one day. Not any man in particular, and I don't mean a UPS man sex fantasy either, but some other future love that wasn't him. Even when we were together.

That sometimes I believe in *the* one, and sometimes I don't, though most of the time when I believe in *the* one I think we've never been guaranteed we'll actually meet this person, or if we do meet, that it can work out—maybe you're moving in two months, already have a boyfriend or wife, are named what I'm named, or maybe I'm just too heartbroken to pay attention to the fact that the guy standing in front of me is you, my one. That, at some point, I realized my imagining another man as a possible future partner, even when I was satisfied with the one I had, meant I was going to be ok. That, at some point, I also realized most of the time when I thought I was talking to the dog, I wasn't really talking to the dog.

That the absolute truth then is there isn't even just one of you. There's a whole crew of possible you's—faces I see around and glance at and act anxious in front of. You are the one with the adorable ears who seems even more nervous than me. You are the one who sings when he dances, who might look a little too much like my ex. You are the one who is so tall and with such wide shoulders that the gentleness of your smile surprises. You are the one with the dark beard, and the laugh that makes your whole serious face break open.

That for a long time, I thought it wasn't possible for two men to love and be happy together forever. That later, I started believing in this kind of love again, even though I'm still not sure it's possible. That I want it to be this way, or else I don't want it.

That on our first date we shouldn't go out for Indian food

because it gives me the flu. That we shouldn't go out for sushi either because I tend to dislike people who like sushi. That I will wear my striped shirt because it makes me feel taller. That I may stare into your face from time to time and think, This is happening! That it would be nice if we could laugh often, and at some point, if you think we're having a good time, it would also be nice for you to smile and tell me so, and then I'll say something like, "We should do this again," and then, at the end of the date, we won't have to wonder what the other one is thinking. That I will want to hear your boyfriend history but will not ask, and this I promise. That sudden silence doesn't always mean awkwardness, sometimes it means ease. That we should split the bill. That you will have to lean in first to kiss me. That if you lean in first to kiss me, I will kiss you back.

You Can't Turn Off
the Snake Light

· · · · ·

We're kissing in my bed, naked and sliding along each
other. My mouth on his neck, his mouth on my
ear. "Say something dirty," he says. It's morning, and we're
fooling around before work, keeping ourselves quiet because my
roommate shuffles on the other side of the wall in the kitchen,
eating cereal. Fooling around before work is new to me. For
that matter, waking up next to a man so many weeks in a row is
new. This is the man who will be my first boyfriend and we'll be
together almost eight years before he decides to leave, but at the
moment, we've only known each other a couple of months. This
is also the first man to call me *his* boyfriend. And now suddenly,
on a Tuesday morning, this man is also the first to ask me to say
something dirty.

The only other thing I've ever been asked to do by a naked
man in a bed was to bite. That man was ten years older than me,
and the first I ever dated after coming out. All over, he said,
stretched out under me on his belly with his arms reaching to
either side. Before that evening, whenever we were in his bed,

or mine, he would ask, gently, "Have you ever done this before?" It never mattered that regardless of whatever we were doing at the moment my answer was always, always *no*, he still asked. "Don't worry about it being too hard," he said, about the biting. "It's never too hard." Below my window then, somewhere in the darkness, a neighbor trudged down the gangway rustling sacks of groceries and dropping the house keys. Candles burned—I thought at that time that being in bed with a man required candlelight—and the jumpy yellow glow might have helped the room not appear like a skimpy-salaried 23 year old's: blank walls, curtainless windows, a spindly nightstand rescued from an alley, a writing desk just a little too small. I leaned over the man's flat back, put my face against the rubbery muscle nestled next to his spine, and pinched him with my teeth. He twitched under me, his head hanging off the mattress. I kept at it, patiently drawing on him parentheses of teethmarks, covering the surface of his skin as though I was running an iron into every corner of a wrinkly shirt.

What I thought about later, after our short time together ended, was that I hadn't considered whether or not I even wanted to bite a man all over his back. I just did it because he asked me and I liked him. So when my first boyfriend makes his request for something dirty, I wish saying it were as easy as biting. Part of it is certainly that the man I bit didn't mean as much to me as the boyfriend does. Even if what I'm feeling so early in our knowing each other isn't all that clear. We've just recently decided to be boyfriends but we haven't made any promises, and the descriptions and definitions of any specific feelings have been left unsaid. I just know I want to be around him as much as possible, and when I see him after not seeing him, I know that my face always comes apart in smiles.

What I don't know right now are any actual dirty words to say. And it's not only that I've never said such words, but also dirty things have never been whispered to me. I haven't even seen much porn for any ideas. Just the one with the two guys working out, one spotting the other at the bench press—the one my boyfriend stole from his roommate's closet, which we watched on his 10" black-and-white TV with the also-borrowed VCR teetering on top. But everything they said was mostly related to exercise.

I pull myself off my boyfriend's chest, and sink into the mattress beside him. I hold his face. We keep kissing. I wrap my ankle behind his and pin us together. Because we're waiting for me to say something—to play along and satisfy the request—the room feels suddenly silent, heavy with the absence, amplifying the sounds we'd normally miss. The bed squeaks under us, the birds peck at the eaves outside the window, our feet skid and shush against the sheets. I suck in air, scoot against the mattress and lift my mouth to his ear.

"I—" is how I begin. Subject, I think, now verb then object. Didn't I graduate almost two years ago with an English degree, didn't I take creative writing classes, wasn't I a copywriter in an ad agency scratching out headlines all day long? This should be easy. "I—" is the next try, more of a way to stall than to repeat for the sake of emphasis. But it also commits me to the pronoun. And I wonder why I always tell people I want to be a writer— how saying things like that makes them expect me to be good at saying things like this. What's the point of dirty talk anyway— isn't it always pretend? Don't we all know that? I should just say something quickly without worrying how it sounds—tame, immature, inexperienced, whatever. We'll be late for work if I don't hurry. Just say something.

"I love you." It comes out in the loudest whisper I'll ever hear.

My friend Tom sits next to me on a stool in our town's only gay bar. The place is dark with black lights and video screens, and crowded with chrome tables. A huge mirror stands like a wallflower next to the dance floor, and a disco ball twirls from the ceiling. Tom sips his whisky neat while I poke the lime at the bottom of my gin, and when the skinny young waiters stamp around in sneakers and $25 underwear, it's difficult not to think of this place as a brilliant but awful cliché of every other gay bar I've ever been in. The entrance is actually in an alley, recalling those old days when gay men had to slink past trashcans to an unmarked door. The music is always too loud so Tom and I have to lean into each other up front where we always sit so we can watch the arrivals—each time the door swings open, we swivel to see who's here, becoming part of the cliché ourselves. Unfortunately it's never anyone cute, which is the point. We end up here every couple of weeks.

"I read an article in *Time* today," I say, close to his ear, over the hammering beat. "It was called 'Are Gay Relationships Different?'" Tom sets down his glass and gives it a small push. "Well of course they are," he says.

"Right." But I don't feel as sure as he seems. "I guess there's something different about the way we argue?" I try, but fail to recall the details of a psychology study the author quoted about common causes for gay male break-ups—not mentioning my own relief that constant nagging and general fussiness were not among them. "And then there's the whole monogamy and promiscuity thing," I say, shrugging, smiling, bringing us to our old favorite argument.

At twenty-five, Tom is eight years younger than me and never lived inside a closet. He wears makeup and a nose ring and cuts his own hair. When I hadn't dated anyone months after my boyfriend dumped me, and I would often announce that I would never date again, not ever, Tom suggested I have a one-night stand. "I think you just need some emotionless sex right now," he told me, and I said I didn't know there was such a thing, at which he shook his head. Another night when we were perched on these stools, we compared numbers. How many men we'd each been with. When I told him my number, he smirked and told me his, which was exactly mine when multiplied by ten.

"Yeah," he said. "You should really have a one-night stand." Being afraid of ending up in some man's deep freezer is my general reply to his goading, and I usually suggest that he should be more careful—the debate quiets there. But once he had the actual statistics, he wouldn't give up. He pointed to a man walking through the door at that moment, a man Tom knew wasn't even my type, and when I wrinkled up my face, he said he'd also throw in twenty bucks. "It's still 'no,'" I said. Then I started laughing. "What now?" he asked. "I miscounted," I said. "I accidentally added one."

A half-naked waiter delivers our next round. He barely looks old enough to serve these drinks, and even though most people mistake me for younger than I really am, I suddenly feel old as he stands in front of me with his hips tilted. Perfect skin, 10 pounds or so underweight. There's nothing the least bit attractive about him, but when I think about myself at his age, every corner of myself stuffed with shame and secret crushes, I can't help but envy him. Where would I be now if I had his confidence then? He hands me change, I give him a dollar. When he's gone, I bring up the magazine again. Even though it didn't ultimately last, I sometimes think of my eight-year run with my ex as a kind of achievement, a credential allowing me to speak on such matters. I ask Tom, "Why are you sure our relationships are different? If love isn't all the same, then how do gay men learn to do it?"

We both think. If we learn to love by trying and failing,

then I wonder how many times it takes before you get it right? Tom answers, "I don't think we do learn. Or we don't just do what straight people do." He brings his glass to his lips but doesn't drink. "I think we re-invent love every time."

And I don't know what to say, I am that surprised.

Tom Brokaw wears a grey suit and speaks to us with a blue wall behind him. I'm sitting on the floor in front of the TV, petting the brown yarn of the shag carpet. My dad dozes on the couch, and in the kitchen, my mom bangs pots. I've already set the table. I'm seven or I'm eight or I'm nine so I don't actually listen to the news because I've tried and don't understand, but it's still something we do before dinner, the same as carrying our plates to the sink once we've eaten, and my brother and I taking our baths when the clock says 8. So I'm coloring or playing with Star Wars guys or reading a library book, waiting for the call to the table, and flashing up on the screen—as it has been now for days or weeks or years?—is AIDS. Four letters I can read but make little sense of, even if it seems to everyone that I've been reading since I was born. The word sounds scary, the serious way Tom Brokaw's lips crimp and his voice slows when he talks about it is scary, as is the way he always says this word with "gay," another one I don't understand.

More than twenty years later, as much as I'll sort through my memory, I won't ever locate my first image of two men in love. But I'll realize that the first gay men I ever saw, the only ones I knew for most of childhood in fact were the dying men on the evening news.

I am a fifth grader, and a boy on the news with the same name as me has AIDS and his school is afraid of him. He got this disease from blood in the hospital—the doctors didn't mean to give it to him—but even so, everyone in his Midwestern town that isn't very far from my Midwestern town—I've asked—is scared to be around him including the other kids and some teachers. And even though his family says he isn't, everybody at his school calls him "gay."

By this point, I've learned the meaning of "gay." After a neighbor showed me a *Playboy* he stole from his dad, and I recoiled at the sight of it, and he told the other boys in our class, and one of them told me I was gay, I asked my mother if that were true. She sat on the edge of my mattress right before bedtime. My room was dark, but the light above the bathroom mirror shined from across the hall. Her face was a shadow. "No," she said, patting my leg through the blankets. "You're not gay." And though she never accused me of anything, I knew it had been wrong to look at the naked women in the magazine and I knew there was something wrong about "gay" based on the way the boys at school and Tom Brokaw talked about it, so I still felt guilty.

Besides that night with my mother and my question, no one in my family ever talked about what gay was. And if AIDS came up, it was because of the news, and the stacks of papers and *Time* forever piling on the living room carpet or kitchen table. One Saturday afternoon, when I was a sixth or seventh grader, we met one of my aunts for lunch at Wendy's, and she whispered that we shouldn't touch the knobs of the restroom doors after washing our hands at the sink because of AIDS. I told her that you couldn't catch it that way, and she shook her head. "They don't really know how it's spread." But this would have been in 1987 or 1988 when they actually did.

Around that time, I remembered that as a six-month old, I'd fallen off the countertop in the kitchen. My head was concussed and my skull was cracked, and the ER doctors kept me in the hospital overnight to track my vital signs. This would have been late December 1975 or early January 1976. Thinking of the other boy with my name, and picturing myself wriggling and screaming on that kitchen floor, I reasoned that I must have received a blood transfusion. It seemed impossible that I hadn't. And I knew that the blood saved in hospitals for such emergencies wasn't tested for HIV in those years because the virus wasn't even around yet. So at the age of thirteen, without any actual evidence, I convinced myself I was HIV positive.

It's difficult to understand why I so easily accepted that fate—why, one might say, I wanted to have AIDS. Because I didn't ever tell anyone about my self-diagnosis—I wasn't looking for sympathy, or all the attention the other Ryan got for his disease. But I knew something separated me from the other boys in my class. Ever since fourth grade, the word "gay" and its harsher synonyms had followed me down school hallways, into lockerrooms and school cafeterias. One afternoon in 8th grade, in the after-lunch rush of boys in the restroom trying to beat the fifth-hour bell, I stood at a urinal. Over the hum of hand dryers and swooshes of flushing, one of my classmates shouted. "Hey, Ryan. Do you ride the cotton pony?" It took a couple of years before I figured out his euphemism, but the fact that my neck still changed from pale to red in about two seconds was all the confirmation he and the others in the room needed. I wasn't a boy like they were, and it was in my blood. Maybe deciding that I had AIDS was the proof I wanted for that difference— something real, measurable and best of all, not my fault.

It's July 25, 2008, and I'm back in Chicago for the weekend. Two years ago, I left this city for a small town—the one with the lone gay bar—and it was there, almost exactly a year after my eight-year boyfriend left me, that I met the new man I'm dating. Before we met, he'd been planning to move to Chicago, and a few months later he did—settling into the same neighborhood I'd left a few years earlier. We hadn't wanted to stop seeing each other, so now we visit back and forth. It says something when you're willing to drive four hours for a glimpse of somebody and people I know call him my "boyfriend," but he and I don't use that word. We can't even bring ourselves to say "relationship." We were both hurt very much the last time.

On this date ten years ago, I came out of the closet, and

we've returned to the site of my admission—a gay bar. Coming out of the closet *in a gay bar* seems sort of beside the point, but for years and years before that big night, I could very easily insist I wasn't gay even while dancing under spinning lights to "Disco Inferno." I used to be a perfect liar.

This new man I'm dating keeps shaking his head, stunned I remember the exact date of my anniversary. This bar is only a few blocks away from his studio apartment, but tonight is the first time he's been inside. The bartender scoots our drinks toward us. He's handsome and tall, probably in his late 40s, and he grins at us in the crooked, devilish way of handsome, tall bartenders in gay bars. He was a bartender here ten years ago, though his eyes are gripped a little deeper now with crow's feet, and the shiny round at the crown of his head has widened. After coming out, I became a regular at this bar and met every man I dated in Chicago here. It's a place full of ghosts. In those days, I wouldn't have needed to order my drink—this bartender would have just seen my empty glass, and fixed me another. I had to actually order tonight, and I'm crestfallen that I wasn't recognized but also relieved. And anyway, my drink has changed.

"So where would you have been ten years ago?" I ask my new guy. It had been a Saturday night. I was 23 at the time, and here with my best friend who was visiting for the weekend. She was the first person I had wanted to tell. In fact, the week before she arrived, as I drove home each evening from my office, I practiced. With the radio turned down, I said aloud, "I am gay. I am gay. I am gay." I wanted to run any quiver out of my voice. In the end, I'd need a couple of drinks to even get started, and we'd have to lock ourselves in the women's restroom so we could cry.

His eyes point to the ceiling and while he thinks, I study his marvelous chin. He's ten years younger than me so he would have been in sixth grade. I squint, picturing his thirteen-year-old self—long limbs, giant feet and his face bare without his beard. This slouching imaginary kid isn't very far in front of his first dates with men and then a bit later, his first real boyfriend—all of it adding up to more experience at 23 than I have now in my thirties because I dragged my feet for so many years, then lived with the same man for most of a decade.

After my break-up, I hated seeing gay male couples, particularly if they looked happy, and especially in the wedding announcement portraits of the Sunday *New York Times*. I was jealous, of course, and angry, and I silently cursed them for having what I was missing. *One of you will leave soon and the other one is too stupid to see it.* I often wondered if I'd ever again believe any man's promises. In my worst moments, I doubted it was possible for two men to ever successfully commit to each other, thinking the bad rap we get for being shallow and promiscuous was true. Naïve as it was, I felt like the solitary romantic, even if couples of all kinds have been messing around with tradition and commitment for decades. The best we could hope for, it seemed in those days, and sometimes still does, was sex every once in a while with mostly bearable periods of loneliness in between.

My new guy scratches his whiskers. "Probably I was at one of my Dad's basketball games, so the high school gym." He shrugs, and I smile because he's just not old enough to be this sentimental. "You ready for the historic tour?" I ask, hopping off my stool. "Grab your beer. I'll show you the *actual* spot." How strange to share this place with a man as old now as I was then, and to realize I never thought about love until I was out of it.

The boa constrictor needs the light on every minute of his life and he curls around it to squeeze the heat with his scales. It's two in the morning, and my boyfriend and I are in the basement bedroom of his nephew, the second of his older brother's three sons; it's the last night of our weekend visit to Ohio. I'm across the room from the boa constrictor's aquarium, stretched out on a threadbare sofa that smells suspiciously like dogs. My boyfriend sleeps on a mattress between the desk holding the boa's aquarium and a wall full of shelves with the other snake, a ball python, the lizard and the scorpion.

Of course at home in Chicago, we sleep together in the bed we've shared for years. I have rules about being touched when I'm trying to fall asleep so we rest sort of shoved against each other with an extra pillow between us that we've named "Brown" for the color of the pillowcase, as in, "Stop hogging 'Brown,' and put him back in the middle, please.'" Before I have the chance to think that it's odd to sleep in a basement with three reptiles and a murderous insect—whatever scorpions are—I realize it probably can't be any stranger than two men sleeping every night with a pillow that has a name.

Under me, the sofa is lumpy but comfortable and covered in worn bed sheets. Despite the light, I'm turned toward the boa, watching him because I can't sleep. The cylindrical bulb hangs over the tangled driftwood inside the aquarium. The snake unfurls his head and slender neck from the tighter mass of himself and pokes around the light, one way and then the other, as though he can't find a good sleeping spot. My boyfriend does the same thing on his borrowed mattress. He shifts under his blanket, wiggles his butt, and by the pace of his breathing, I know he's awake.

"Hey," I whisper across the darkness. He replies with more wiggling and a deep short groan—the sound he makes in the middle of the night when one of us rolls out of a dream and bumps the other or he wakes up freezing because I've stolen the quilt. It means he isn't fully asleep but neither is he awake. As soon as I hear that little grunt in this basement, and away from the privacy of our bedroom, it feels wrong.

I whisper, "No," but now he's gone, fallen into real sleep, simply and unnoticed, as usual. He needs to lie still for only about a minute in order to sleep soundly for eight hours. My slumber is more conditional and involves complete darkness and silence, and the following items: a glass of water, tissues, my cell phone, and Chapstick. Right now, it's all balanced on a weight bench next to the sofa.

My boyfriend's brother knows about us. His wife also knows because he told her after my boyfriend came out to him. We don't know if the boys know, and my boyfriend hasn't found the right moment this weekend to ask. They're all teenagers so it seems that they probably figured it out on their own. Why else would their uncle keep bringing his roommate to family barbecues, graduations and anniversary parties?

One of the boys is watching a movie upstairs on the big TV next to the tank with the piranhas. It's something loud about robots; mechanical voices and machine squeaks drift down the stairs. Tomorrow morning, we're getting up early to drive the six hours of barns and trees back home. I shove my shoulder down into the cushion and knead the pillow with my cheek, still facing the snake light. I thought the sofa was keeping me awake, but hearing the soft, familiar snore across the room, I think I'm not used to sleeping like this—in the same room with him but not *with* him. Even if I usually can't fall asleep with him touching me, there's something so lonely about the room, this sofa, that snake.

I could sleep with him. Just get up and in that bed and no one would ever know, and it could be as easy as tiptoeing across the carpet, sliding under the blanket and into my place on his left side. But what if his nephew needs something in the morning, tries to sneak in for a T-shirt, or to feed his zoo, and sees us, in *his* bed? Then I remember my boyfriend's brother— the kid's dad—never said we had to sleep separately. When he showed us his son's room where we'd sleep for the weekend, he first demonstrated how to keep out the dogs by wedging a dumbbell against the door, and then he nodded to the far corner of the room, at the aquarium on the desk.

"The only thing is," he said. "You can't turn off that light."

"The light for that snake has to stay on all night?" I asked, too loudly.

"Yeah, you can't turn off the snake light," he said, shrugging.

My boyfriend and I had separated ourselves automatically, without a word between us or for any good reason.

So how do we learn to be in love? My friend Michael has no answer except to say that's some heavy thinking. My friend Brian isn't sure he wants to answer because he's afraid of sounding like a cliché, or worse, an old, old man. But when he does, he remembers his first boyfriend, both of them eighteen, both of them stepping out of their closets and into each other's lives. And he cringes at what he considered romantic back then— cheesy poems, piano serenades, feeding each other. But think about hetero kids, he says. They get to start dating when they're twelve, so we shouldn't feel bad about being corny because we were making up for lost time. Andrew says old movies. Jordan doesn't think he ever learned how to be in love with a man. I treat my boyfriends like buddies, he says, because friendship with guys is the only model there is. And how does that usually work out? He laughs, and says one word: disappointing. Paul says watching his parents. He learned about commitment and fidelity from how his mom stuck with his dad no matter what. Kevin doesn't have any idea but thinks it's ironic that pretty much the only time we get to see two gay men doing anything together is in porn, and those construction crews and corrals of cowboys aren't very affectionate. About my question, Landon just says that it's interesting.

My ex-boyfriend, the one who left me after eight years, who lives now with his new boyfriend says my question is hard. "I know," I say, and I'm not sure if he means it's a difficult one, or it's difficult because I'm the one asking. "I think for me learning to fall in love with a man came from instinct," he says. I don't want him to think that I'm asking about us so I make my voice sound like a newscaster's—the steady tone, whether they're delivering good or bad news. "What instinct?" "For completeness," he says. "After coming out it was easier because the secrecy was gone." Before that, it could have been anyone, it didn't matter who, it was always only fooling around. "Has that instinct been revised?" I ask before I think enough about it. I'm not sure I should hear his answer, and then I wonder if his new relationship is more likely to last because he learned from our failure. "Yes," he says. "It's less about emotions now," and he smiles quietly. "And more about commitment." Does that answer the question?

———

After my ex moved in with his new boyfriend, and we were trying to be friends, my best friend Margaret told me she didn't understand. "All the gay men I know stay close with their exes." She's divorced and would be happy to never hear from *that* man again. "Isn't that hard?" I'd just told her the latest thing my ex had mentioned during a phone conversation that I had taken personally. "I don't know why you'd want to hear that," she said. I wanted to say, but didn't, that I was probably still in love with him. And I wanted to say, but didn't, that strange as it was, there was something comforting in how our past loves collaborate with our present. And I wanted to say, but also didn't, that spending so much time feeling ashamed of who we are must bear on the ways we love each other—it just has to. But I wasn't sure, so I told her I didn't want to let go because finding love with a man has been so rare and hard.

I'm in bed with him, the new man, my face on his back, thinking about that conversation with her months before this night, and the only thing I know about love is that I don't know anything. Whatever I've learned is lost when we're like this, and I'm falling asleep against him in the spot where I'll wake in the morning, when he'll leave for another month of us away from each other. "What are we doing?" is the question always under everything, the one I can't ask. One answer could be "reinventing love," but that's only one. Tonight, we've had dinner at the place where we always have dinner. We've eaten cookie dough Blizzards—he insisted we order the largest size as he always does. We've curled together on the sofa, easing into each other and sleep, before bed. *What are we doing?* Not one of us knows.

I push my chest into his back, tuck my knees into the crook of his bent knees. My mouth only a few inches behind his neck so I can smell his shampoo. Lying on my side, I curl one arm over him and he squeezes my hand in his. My other arm slides under the pillow under his head, and shoves forward across the mattress. It's the perfect way to sleep with a man, yet it still feels new every single time. But as soon as my body slides into place, fitting the way that only one key's grooves are carved smooth for only one lock, a memory opens for the first time in ten years. Another bed, another man, another pillow, another back. That older guy I dated, the one who asked for the bites, he taught me this, word by patient word. Put your arm here, he said, tugging my wrist. Push this one under. Scoot closer. Closer. Now pull your knees into me. There. That's it.

RYAN VAN METER grew up in Missouri and studied English at the University of Missouri-Columbia. After graduating, he lived in Chicago for ten years and worked in advertising. He holds an MA in creative writing from DePaul University and an MFA in nonfiction writing from The University of Iowa. His essays have appeared in *The Gettysburg Review, Indiana Review, Gulf Coast, Arts & Letters,* and *Fourth Genre,* among others, and selected for anthologies including *Best American Essays 2009.* In the summer of 2009, he was awarded a residency at the MacDowell Colony. He currently lives in California where he is an assistant professor of creative nonfiction at The University of San Francisco.